100 WALKS IN
COUNTY DURHAM

THE CROWOOD PRESS

First published in 2017 by
The Crowood Press Ltd
Ramsbury, Marlborough
Wiltshire SN8 2HR

www.crowood.com

British Library Cataloguing-in-Publication Data
A catalogue record for this book is available from the British Library.

ISBN 978 1 78500 306 6

Front cover: Shutterstock

Mapping in this book is sourced from the following products: OS Explorer 304, 305, 307, 308,
OL31
© Crown copyright 2016 Ordnance Survey. Licence number 100038003

Every effort has been made to ensure the accuracy of this book. However, changes can occur
during the lifetime of an edition. The Publishers cannot be held responsible for any errors or
omissions or for the consequences of any reliance on the information given in this book, but
should be very grateful if walkers could let us know of any inaccuracies by writing to us at
the address above or via the website.

As with any outdoor activity, accidents and injury can occur. We strongly advise readers to
check the local weather forecast before setting out and to take an OS map. The Publishers
accept no responsibility for any injuries which may occur in relation to following the walk
descriptions contained within this book.

Typeset by Jean Cussons Typesetting, Diss, Norfolk
Printed and bound in India by Replika Press Pvt Ltd

Contents

How to Use this Book

The walks in the book are ordered regionally, and then by distance within each region, starting with the shortest and ending with the longest. An information panel for each walk shows the distance, start point (see below), a summary of level of difficulty (easy/moderate/difficult/strenuous), OS map(s) required, and suggested pubs/cafés at the start/end of walk or on the way. An introductory sentence at the beginning of each walk briefly describes the route and terrain.

Readers should be aware that starting point postcodes have been supplied for satnav purposes and are not indicative of exact locations. Some start points are so remote that there is no postcode.

Maps

There are 92 maps covering the 100 walks. Some of the walks are extensions of existing routes and the information panel for these walks will tell you the distance of the short and long versions of the walk, depending on whether you wish to combine two walks or tackle each singly.

The routes marked on the maps are punctuated by a series of numbered waypoints. These relate to the same numbers shown in the walk description.

Start Points

The start of each walk is given as a postcode and also a six-figure grid reference number prefixed by two letters (which indicates the relevant square on the National Grid). More information on grid references is found on Ordnance Survey maps.

Parking

Many of the car parks suggested are public, but for some walks you will have to park on the roadside or in a lay-by. Please be considerate when leaving your car and do not block access roads or gates. Also, if parking in a pub car park for the duration of the walk, please try to avoid busy times.

Countryside Code

- Consider the local community and other people enjoying the outdoors
- Leave gates and property as you find them and follow paths
- Leave no trace of your visit and take litter home
- Keep dogs under effective control
- Plan ahead and be prepared
- Follow advice and local signs

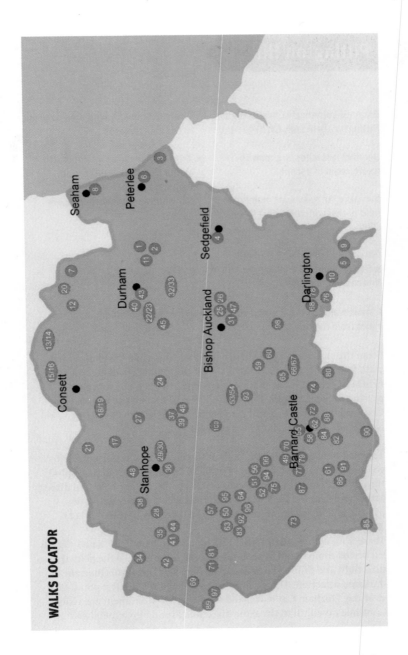

WALKS LOCATOR

Pittington Hill

START St Laurence's Church, High
Pittington, DH6 1AB, GR NZ328435

DISTANCE 2¾ miles/4.4km with
340ft/103m of ascent

SUMMARY An easy walk mainly along
field paths, with one short steep
climb

MAPS OS Explorer 308 Durham
& Sunderland; OS Landranger 88
Newcastle upon Tyne

PARKING Small parking area adjacent
to the church gates

WHERE TO EAT AND DRINK Hallgarth
Manor Hotel, High Pittington,
T0191-372-1188
www.hallgarthmanorhotel.com

A short walk around the environs of Pittington Hill, with great panoramic
views from the top.

From the church go right along a footpath alongside the churchyard
wall, follow this downhill, cross a footbridge and continue across the
fields to Littletown Farm. Enter the farmyard via a gate and go left,
passing in front of some houses, and then along the track to reach
Coalford La. Cross this and turn right for a short distance to reach a
track leading into Pittington Woods **(1)**.

Turn left here and follow the path until you reach a track on the left;
go down this to cross a bridge. Continue in the same direction uphill
through the conifer plantation to reach another minor road. Go directly
across and take the path which climbs steeply through the woods,
passing an old quarry on the left to reach the edge of the wood **(2)**.

There is no defined path across Pittington Hill from here, so go slightly
left across some rough grass until you reach the edge of the field, then
turn right and follow the field edge; where this stops, continue ahead in
the same direction. There are great views from the highest point: on a
clear day Durham Cathedral and the Penshaw Monument are visible.
Continue downhill in the same direction, aiming for a metal gate at

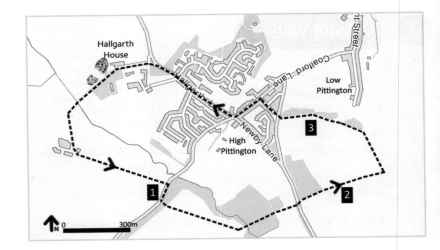

the bottom of the field. Don't go through this; turn left and double back slightly to reach a stile through the hedge. Follow the path through the woods to another stile, cross this and continue in the same direction. Shortly after exiting the woods you will come to a fork in the path (**3**).

Take the right-hand fork and head downhill to reach a metal kissing gate, which gives access onto a minor road. Turn right and then go left down a road between houses to reach Coalford La again. Turn left and walk through the village to the crossroads, here turning right onto Hallgrath La. Follow this past the school, opposite the Hallgarth Manor Hotel. Where the road bends right, keep left and go down the lane towards St Laurence's Church to reach the car park.

Points of interest

Sheltered by a grove of elm and sycamore, the village of High Pittington was once the country retreat of the Prior of the Abbey of Durham.

St Laurence's Church contains a Norman font, which was once sold for half a crown and used as a feeding trough at Belmont Farm; it was rediscovered in 1885 after 76 years.

Cassop Vale

Start Cassop Community Centre, Cassop, DH6 4RP, GR NZ344383

Distance 3¼ miles/5.2km with 400ft/120m of ascent

Summary An easy walk mainly along field paths, with some climbing

Maps OS Explorer 308 Durham & Sunderland; OS Landranger 88 Newcastle upon Tyne

Parking Roadside parking outside the community centre

Where to eat and drink None

A short walk around the environs of Cassop Vale and the nature reserve.

From the community centre walk past the entrance to the nature reserve and continue along the B6291 until it starts to curve left. Leave the road at the footpath sign on the right and head across two fields to Cassop Hill farm, pass behind the farm, and continue in the same direction to reach the radio mast **(1)**.

Go right onto a track and follow this through woods and dolomite outcrops to reach a wooden gate/stile. Cross this and join a track coming in from the right. Follow this downhill through two more gates/stiles. At the bottom of the hill go right and then left after a short distance. Cross a stream and exit the woods via a gate, and cross the field to reach a fenced area with a number of gates **(2)**.

Turn left and exit the enclosed area, crossing the field to reach a stile that gives access onto a fenced lane. Follow this until you reach an open area, keeping right along the track as it starts to climb up the hill to eventually reach a minor road. Turn right and follow this into Old Cassop village. Walk through the village to where the road turns 90 degrees left **(3)**.

Leave the road and go through the farmyard, which gives access to a fenced lane. Follow the lane as it climbs over the hill – there are good views of the vale from here. There's a small dogleg right in the path where its starts to descend back into Cassop Vale. At the bottom of the hill you will reach the same enclosed area as earlier in the walk **(2)**. Take the stile on the left, behind the seat, and follow the track back towards Cassop village, walking through the nature reserve. Just after passing the lake the path begins to climb, reaching a road beside the water treatment works. Go left and follow this uphill to reach the village a short distance from the community centre.

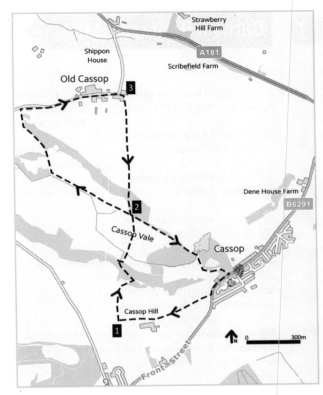

Points of interest

Cassop Vale was once the bed of a shallow lagoon, into which flowed rivers carrying large amounts of calcium and magnesium salts. When the waters evaporated in the high temperatures of that time vast deposits of dolomite and calcium were created. Distortions of the earth's crust raised this dolomite sea-bed, which retreating glaciers ripped and serrated. Man has quarried it extensively, farmed its topsoil and mined through it looking for coal.

Durham Heritage Coast

START Crimdon Beach car park, Hartlepool, TS27 4BW, GR NZ481372

FINISH Limekiln Gill car park, Horden, SR8 4HN, GR NZ454406

DISTANCE 3¼ miles/5.2km with 350ft/120m of ascent

SUMMARY An easy walk along the clifftop paths, with some steps

MAPS OS Explorer 308 Durham & Sunderland; OS Landranger 88 Newcastle upon Tyne

PARKING Clifftop car park beside the holiday park

WHERE TO EAT AND DRINK None

A linear walk along the clifftops of the Durham Heritage Coast.

Take the coastal path north from the car park. Initially this runs alongside the holiday park and you will pass close to the caravans which look out to sea. Where the tarmac path runs out, keep on over grass following the clifftop path. Soon after leaving the holiday park the path is forced away from the sea by a deep inlet; follow the path to reach a tunnel under the railway **(1)**.

Don't go through the tunnel, but turn right and go through a gate and follow the path. There is a detour to the route indicated on the OS map at this point, due to coastal erosion. Follow the new fence line until you reach a set of steps descending to the right; go down these and up the other side. Continue along the clifftop path – there is now no fence so caution is needed as the cliffs are unstable and steep. Keep right as you reach a car park, briefly joining a surfaced track. The path continues on to reach a notice board at the steps at Blackhall Rocks. Don't descend these, but keep left along the clifftop path.

Soon after reaching the inlet of Blue House Gill, the path is forced inland again, joining another surfaced track at the location of the old Blackhall Colliery. Turn left and join this track for a short distance **(2)**, leaving it where the coastal path turns right, heading back to the clifftops. Where the path passes some allotment gardens, away to your left, ignore any tracks heading towards them. Keep on the clifftop path to reach some black metal posts at the top of some steps (good views here of the railway viaduct over Castle Eden Dene). Go down the steps into the valley below. After crossing the stream via the footbridge keep right to round Hartlepool Point, and then go left into Limekiln Gill, following the path to reach the car park.

Note: it is possible to return to the start of the walk along the clifftop path, or alternatively if the tide is low you can walk all the way back along the beach. But please take care as this is only possible at low tide; the section south of Blackhall Rocks would be impassable when the tide is in. Also note that many of the steps up/down from the beach indicated on the OS maps are no longer usable due to landslips.

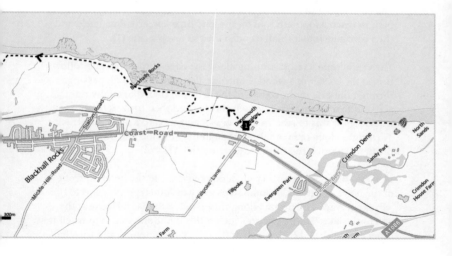

Hardwick Park

START Hardwick Park Visitor Centre, TS21 2EH, GR NZ345287

DISTANCE 3½ miles/5.6km with 270ft/80m of ascent

SUMMARY An easy walk mainly along field paths and tracks

MAPS OS Explorer 308 Durham & Sunderland; OS Landranger 88 Newcastle upon Tyne

PARKING Pay and display car parking

WHERE TO EAT AND DRINK The Tower Café, by the visitor centre T01740-621505 (open 10–4)

A pleasant walk in country parkland and surrounding fields.

From the visitor centre go left along the track signposted 'to dog exercise area', running alongside a fence. Serpentine Lake can be seen through the trees on the right, which you will walk around later in the walk. Continue along the track to the far end to reach a gate, go through this and turn right onto another track and then right again onto a downhill path to reach a footpath sign on the left. Turn left, crossing a field and then continue into a small wooded area to reach a gate (**1**).

Turn right onto a track running along the edge of the field, and follow this to the corner of a wood. Continue alongside the wood, passing through the gate in the corner of the field and then diagonally right across it to a footbridge. Cross the bridge and then turn right onto a track; follow this to reach a large gravel area next to a quad bike track. Turn right along the road, keep right at the junction and pass behind the hotel to reach the entrance gates on the A177 (**2**).

Don't go through these; go right along the drive to the hotel. In front of the hotel, go left down some steps to a gate which gives access to the 'Grand Terrace'. Turn right along this, passing the Bath House at the end of the lake. The path then goes left through Bono Retiro to reach the other side of the lake. Keep left at the next path junction, and then left at

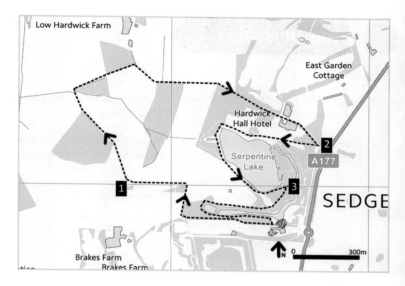

the following one, which will take you down onto the path between the lake and Fen Carr (**3**).

Go right over the wooden walkway over the boggy ground of Fen Carr and then right at the next junction to reach Serpentine Bridge. You could go directly back to the car park by crossing the bridge at this point, or keep straight on to follow the loop path around the lake.

Points of interest

Hardwick Park is a country park with a difference. It has survived since the 1750s when its then owner, John Burdon, created a sprawling ornamental park. He enhanced the ornamental lake on the south side of the hall by adding an artificial river leading to it and encircling it with a walkway. In all, he laid out forty acres of additional ornamental features, including temples, grottoes and follies, designed primarily by London architect James Paine. Although the grounds and buildings were not subsequently well maintained, the garden retains the basic structure put into place by Paine and is an unusual example of authentic eighteenth-century landscape design.

Low Dinsdale

START The Front, Middleton One Row, DL2 1AS, GR NZ352123

DISTANCE 6 miles/9.7km with 275ft/83m of ascent

SUMMARY An easy walk mainly along riverside and field paths

MAPS OS Explorer 304 Darlington & Richmond; OS Landranger 93 Middlesbrough

PARKING Roadside parking opposite The Devonport Hotel

WHERE TO EAT AND DRINK Gabriella's Coffee Shop, in The Devonport Hotel, T01325-332255, www.devonporthotel.co.uk (open Mon–Sat 9–5)

A pleasant walk along the lower reaches of the River Tees to the medieval village of Low Dinsdale.

From The Front, which is beautifully sited some 60ft above the River Tees, go diagonally right, down across a grassy slope towards the woods/river. Keep right at the bottom, heading upstream along the riverside path to reach a parking area at the end of a lane. Go left through the gates and along the road towards the house at the end (1).

Pass in front of the house to enter a wooded area, then keep on the good path through the woods, which gives glimpses of the river down to the left. Ignore any paths going off uphill on the right, continuing on to reach a gate after about a mile. Leave the woods through the gate and go directly across the field, heading towards the church at Low Dinsdale (2).

On reaching the road opposite the church, turn right and walk through the village, continuing until a gate/footpath sign is reached on the right beneath some trees. Go right into the field and follow the path along the right-hand side, continuing alongside the edge of the woods until you reach the golf course. Here, the path turns right and cuts across the golf course; the way is well defined, but note the warnings about golf balls (3).

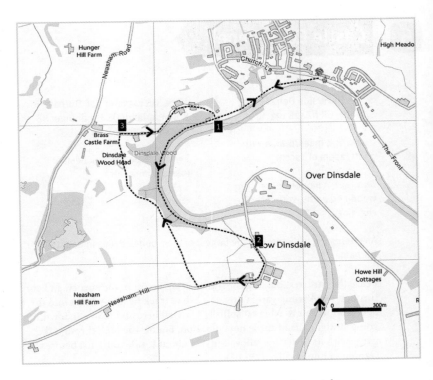

Upon reaching the road at the other side of the course, turn right, following the road into Dinsdale Park. Go between the houses and then onto a lane heading down through the trees to reach the riverside again (1). The return to Middleton One Row is back along the riverside path, retracing the outward part of the walk.

Points of interest

Historically, Low Dinsdale was commonly known as Dinsdale. The 'Low' was added to distinguish the village from the neighbouring village of Over Dinsdale, on the opposite bank of the River Tees in North Yorkshire. The name is Old English and means 'nook of land belonging to a man named Dyttin or Deighton'.

Castle Eden Dene

Start Oakerside Dene Lodge, SR8 1NJ, GR NZ428393

Distance 4 miles/6.4km with 730ft/220m of ascent

Summary A moderate walk on woodland paths, with lots of climbing

Maps OS Explorer 308 Durham & Sunderland; OS Landranger 88 Newcastle upon Tyne

Parking Free car park beside information centre

Where to eat and drink None

An interesting walk through the largest of the wooded denes in County Durham.

Leave the car park, passing the information board in the corner, and go through two kissing gates to reach a broad track heading down into the dene; follow this to where it splits (**1**). Go left here and follow it downhill, going straight ahead at the next junction. Follow the path through the gorge with its towering yellow cliffs for about a mile until just before the Garden of Eden bridge (**2**).

The dene is a steep-sided valley that was cut into the magnesian limestone of east Durham by the glacial meltwaters. Subsequent glacial activity covered the area in thick deposits of boulder clay. This makes the slopes of the dene very unstable and frequent landslides can occur, exposing the limestone in places. Don't cross this bridge; go right on an uphill path which climbs steeply for a while to reach a seat. Keep right to reach a wooden fence/stile beside a notice board. Don't cross this, but turn right and follow the path alongside the fence/edge of the woods until you reach a cross track. Turn right and follow the track downhill to another track junction beside a stream (**3**).

Go right here downhill for a short distance, then go left at the next junction, following the track uphill to reach a metal gate close to The Castle. Turn right and follow the path alongside the fence until the path splits; turn right downhill. At the bottom turn left to join a track and continue to reach Gunners Pool Bridge (**4**).

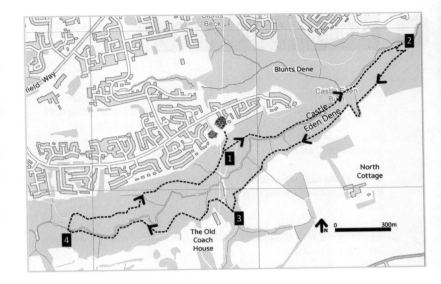

Cross the bridge and climb steeply uphill. At the top go right and follow the path through the woods. Keep right at the next two junctions and then go left at the third to climb back to reach the outward route (**1**). Go left uphill back to the car park.

Points of interest

Castle Eden Dene is a magical place full of legend and folklore, which has been left to spread and sprawl through the deep wooded gorge over hundreds of years. It is now the largest area of unspoilt natural woodland in the North-east of England, famous for its majestic yew trees and fantastic stands of ancient oak and ash.

WALK

7 Lumley Park and Castle

START Lumley Riverside Park,
DH3 4NT, GR NZ282508

DISTANCE 4¾ miles/7.6km with
320ft/100m of ascent

SUMMARY An easy walk mainly
through woods and along riverside
paths

MAPS OS Explorer 308 Durham
& Sunderland; OS Landranger 88
Newcastle upon Tyne

PARKING Pay and display car parking

WHERE TO EAT AND DRINK None

An interesting walk through woods, with good views of riverside and park,
best done in spring.

From the car park entrance turn left and cross the River Wear via
Lumley New Bridge and walk along the footpath beside the B1284 to
Castle Dene – lovely views here of Lumley Castle through the trees (**1**).
At the roundabout take the second exit on the left onto Forge La. Follow
this as it passes under the A1 motorway and then over Lumley Park
Burn, before climbing the steps on the left, cutting the corner off the
road. Take the first track on the left, cross the motorway again, this time
via a footbridge, to reach Lumley Park Farm. Pass this and continue
along the path into Lumley Park Woods to reach a track junction (**2**).

Continue in the same direction on a good path through the woods, to
reach Lamb Bridge on your left. Don't cross this; stay on the same side
of the stream and continue until you come to Garden House. Go into
the yard in front of the cottage and take the passage to the right of it. Go
through a gate and continue down to reach the stream again. Go right
and walk alongside the stream until you come to a T-junction. Go right
here, uphill, crossing a wooden fence and then across the field to reach a
kissing gate beside the motorway. Go through this and follow the track
over the motorway, passing cottages to reach the A183. Turn left and
walk along the footpath to reach Lambton Bridge (**3**).

After crossing the bridge go immediately left down onto the riverside
path, and walk upstream passing under the A1 again. Continue along

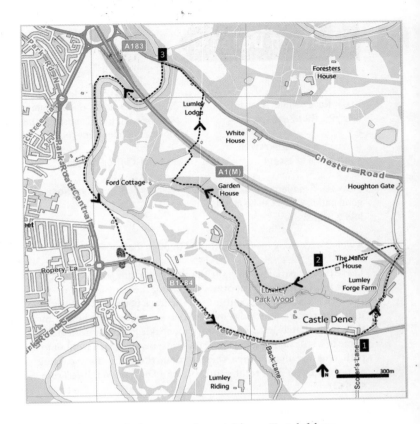

this path until you reach the corner of a metal fence. Turn left here, staying on the riverside path, and follow it back to Lumley Park, crossing a footbridge over Longburn en route.

Points of interest

 Lumley New Bridge was built in 1914 to replace a ferry and toll footbridge.

Lumley Castle was built in the fourteenth century, but reconstructed in 1721 by Sir John Vanburgh, the architect of Blenheim Palace.

Hawthorn Dene

START Nose's Point, Seaham,
SR7 7PS, GR NZ436479

DISTANCE 5 miles/8km with
500ft/150m of ascent

SUMMARY A moderate walk on mainly
good paths, which can be muddy;
lots of steps!

MAPS OS Explorer 308 Durham
& Sunderland; OS Landranger 88
Newcastle upon Tyne

PARKING Clifftop car park

WHERE TO EAT AND DRINK None

A varied walk along the coast path and through the wooded dene.

Leave the car park and go right along the path alongside the fence.
Leave this path and go left over a footbridge, keeping left to go
through a kissing gate. Continue on the track beside the railway line
until you reach a footbridge over it (**1**). Go right over the bridge and
then immediately left, and continue alongside the track until you
come to a stile on the left. Don't cross this; instead, turn right onto a
path, crossing an open area, then continue through woods, passing
an open area on your right, until you see a Durham Wildlife Trust
sign (**2**).

Continue along the path in the same direction until the end of the open
area. Keep on straight ahead along the right-hand edge of the fields until
you reach a second Durham Wildlife Trust sign. Turn left and follow a
muddy path through the woods, with wooden steps in places. This path
winds its way through the woods to return to the first DWT sign that
you passed earlier (**2**). Turn right and retrace your outward route back to
the footbridge over the railway (**1**).

Here, go straight ahead across open ground to reach the clifftop path,
turn left and follow the path to the top of some rocky steps leading down
to the beach. Go right down these and at the bottom go left to walk back
along the beach towards the car park. At the end of the beach there is a
steep path up the cliffs to reach the car park.

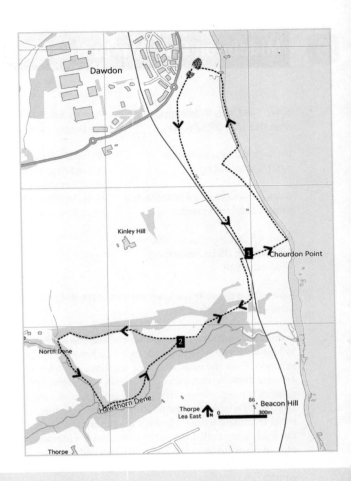

Points of interest

Nose's Point/Blast Beach: Nose's Point and thereabouts have seen ironworks, a bottle factory and a chemical works built, thrive and demolished over the years – as well as, of course, Dawdon Colliery, which closed in 1991. Add to this mix random railways and a ballast dumping ground for merchant ships, and it is a wonder that this area looks as scenic as it does today.

Middleton One Row to Newsham Hall

START The Front, Middleton One Row, DL2 1AS, GR NZ352123

DISTANCE 6 miles/9.7km with 275ft/83m of ascent

SUMMARY An easy walk mainly along riverside and field paths

MAPS OS Explorer 304 Darlington & Richmond; OS Landranger 93 Middlesbrough

PARKING Roadside parking opposite The Devonport Hotel

WHERE TO EAT AND DRINK Gabriella's Coffee Shop, in The Devonport Hotel, T01325-332255 www.devonporthotel.co.uk (open Mon–Sat 9–5)

A pleasing walk along the lower reaches of the River Tees, with good views across to the Cleveland Hills.

From The Front, head towards the eastern end of the village until you see a footpath sign, just before the road junction. Take the path, which goes behind some houses, keeping between them and the river on your right, and passing through some of the gardens via gates and steps. Descend the well-worn path to reach the river behind the water treatment works. The path now continues along the field edge parallel to the river. There is a wide variety of wild plants to be found along the water edges: rosebay willow herb, Himalayan balsam, and giant hogweed to name a few.

As you approach the end of the riverside path, Low Middleton Hall, one-time residence of Sir James Duff, Lieutenant of County Durham, comes into view. Gathered around it like children around a schoolmistress is the small community of Low Middleton. Just after passing the ancient dovecote in the field to your left, the path leaves the riverbank and heads left along the field edge (**1**) to reach a minor road beside the white farm buildings (**5**).

Turn right onto a farm track, crossing a couple of fields before climbing up onto Fatten Hill, from where there are fine views across the Tees valley and of the Cleveland Hills. Keep on the track until you reach some gates, and keep left along the track heading for the farm buildings of Newsham Grange. When you arrive at the farm, pass the farm buildings to reach the farm access road, turn left and follow the minor road (2).

Keep following the road, passing Newsham Hall and House on your left and the ancient medieval village of Newsham in the fields to your right. There are stunning panoramic views across the meandering River Tees towards the Cleveland Hills from here. Just after this, at a road junction (3), turn left to follow the quiet country lane for 1½ miles back to Low Middleton, where you will join the Teesdale Way (5). Roughly half way along the road a signpost on the right (4) leads about 1 mile across the fields to the medieval church of St George's, which provides a worthwhile extension to the route if church architecture is your thing.

The return to Middleton One Row is back along the riverside path from (1), retracing the outward part of the walk.

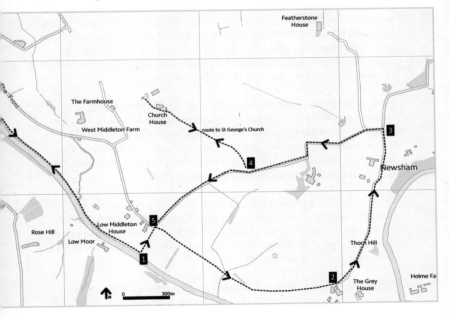

Croft-on-Tees and Stapleton

START Oxen-le-Fields, DL2 2SE,
GR NZ285104

DISTANCE 6 miles/9.7km with
325ft/98m of ascent

SUMMARY An easy walk mainly along
field paths, with some road walking

MAPS OS Explorer 304 Darlington
& Richmond; OS Landranger 93
Middlesbrough

PARKING Roadside parking in lay-by
on the A167

WHERE TO EAT AND DRINK None

A walk of varied character along two loops of the Teesdale Way.

From the lay-by, walk along the track towards Oxen-le-Fields. Just before
the buildings a path heads off left across the field. Cross a stile and then
cross the next field to enter a wooded area; Hells Kettles are on the left of
the wood. Go through the wood to emerge beside North Oxen-le-Fields.
Go to the left of the buildings, joining a track for a short distance until
you reach a footpath marker on the right. Go right along the path to
reach the edge of the golf course. Continue in the same direction along
the road through the course to reach the entrance (1).

Here, turn left along the road to reach the busy Blands Corner
roundabout. Walk towards the garage, crossing the A167 and then the
A66, and go left along the A66 towards Blackwell village. Stay on the
footpath alongside the A66 until you reach Blackwell Bridge over the
River Tees. Here, cross the road and walk along to the roundabout, take
the first left and continue to Stapleton village (2).

In the village take the first road on the left, which will take you first
through the houses and then to Stapleton Grange about a mile further
on. Pass to the left of the buildings, leaving the road and joining a track
along the edge of the fields. There are good views out over the fields in all
directions from this section (3).

Eventually you will come to a wooden gate; go through the gate and
then go left downhill through the trees to reach the river. Go right

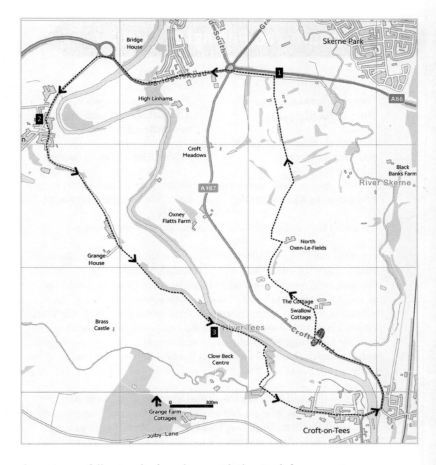

downstream, following the fence line, until Clow Beck forces you to turn right. Follow the beck upstream to the old packhorse bridge at Monk End Farm. Go left over the bridge, passing the large steel floodgates which protect Croft village when the river is in flood. Continue into the farmyard. Go directly through the yard to join a rough track, following this across the fields to the outskirts of the village. Continue through the village along the road until you see the church on the junction with the A167. Go left over Croft Bridge, keeping on the footpath along the A167 until you reach the River Skerne, and continue along the grass verge back to the lay-by.

Sherburn and Pittington Circular

START Sherburn Leisure Centre, DH6 1QX, GR NZ3154237

DISTANCE 9½ miles/15.3km with 810ft/245m of ascent

SUMMARY An easy walk mainly along field paths and woodland tracks

MAPS OS Explorer 308 Durham & Sunderland; OS Landranger 88 Newcastle upon Tyne

PARKING Leisure Centre car park

WHERE TO EAT AND DRINK The Lambton Arms, Sherburn T0191-372-2973

A pleasant walk along paths linking several former mining villages.

From the car park, walk back out onto the main road through the village. Turn left and go to the mini roundabout, then turn left, cross the road and go right along School La. Continue along the road as far as a footpath sign on the left. Take the path across the fields, go right in front of the trees and then left over the footbridge to reach High Pittington church. Take the path on the right alongside the wall and go over the footbridge to Littletown Farm. Keep on in the same direction uphill along the lane, then left across the field to reach the road at Littletown **(1)**.

Go across the road and turn left to walk through the village. At the end go left between garages and downhill into the woods, keeping left to follow the path through Dog Kennel Wood. Shortly after passing Elemore Grange Farm, you reach a footbridge. Go over this and then right to a stile at the edge of the wood. Go right over the stile, then continue along the left-hand edge of the field to join a lane leading up to the farm on the hill **(2)**.

On reaching the farm, go left over a stile to pass the farmyard, then downhill over two fields to cross Coldwell Burn. After crossing this, go steeply uphill along a path to reach the edge of the wood. Turn left and follow the edge of the wood to a track. Turn right and follow this to the village of Hetton-le-Hill. Go left in the village to reach a minor road **(3)**. Cross the road and go right for a short distance to a footpath marker on the left. Turn left here and follow the path along the edge of the field, then right at the hedge, passing a radar station, and then right downhill through woods to High Moorsley (**4**).

Go diagonally right across the road, cross the field downhill to a track, turn left and follow it. Go straight across the road and continue in the same direction to a metal gate. Go through the gate and then right over a stile through the hedge and into a wooded area, continuing to the next gate. Here, go right downhill into Low Pittington village. Walk through the village, keeping right at the junction to reach a crossroads beside a pub (**5**).

Turn left and go along the road to a footpath marker on the right. Go right to join an old railway line and follow this until you reach a bridge over it, bearing left on a path which parallels the other railway line, until you come to some houses. Go behind these, passing some allotments, to reach the leisure centre.

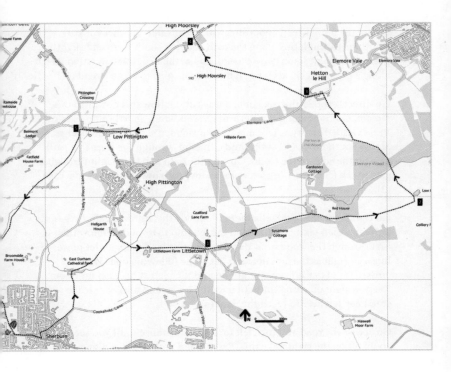

START North Fell car park,
DH2 3RY, GR NZ249498

DISTANCE 3 miles/4.8km with
260ft/80m of ascent

SUMMARY Easy walk mainly along
heath/woodland tracks, which can
be confusing in places

MAPS OS Explorer 307 Consett &
Derwent Reservoir; OS Landranger
88 Newcastle upon Tyne

PARKING Picnic area car park

WHERE TO EAT AND DRINK None

A short walk around the heathlands and woodlands of Waldridge Fell.

From the picnic area walk back out of the entrance and cross the road,
taking the path directly opposite, which leads into another car park.
Continue through this along the path heading south. Descend slightly,
passing through some gorse bushes, and at the next track junction go left
along a grassy track, keeping right where it splits to reach a road (1).

Go directly across the road onto a track and follow this downhill to a
stream. Go right along a path through woodland. Shortly after passing
Brass Castle Farm, go right down steep wooden steps to a footbridge
across South Burn. Cross this and climb up through the trees to a path/
gate on the edge of the wood. Go over the path and then right through a
gate in the fence, turning left to follow the path over two fields to a road
(2).

Go right and walk along the footpath beside this until just after crossing
a stream, then take a footpath on the left into the woods. Follow this, at
first through the woods and then across heathland, pass under power
lines, go right at the junction and left at the following one (3). At a
crossroads of paths keep straight on and then left at the next junction.
Keep straight on along the path over the heathland until you reach a
seat; keep left here to reach the road (4).

Go across the road and turn left for a short distance until you see a track
going off on the right; take this. Pass a pond and continue along until

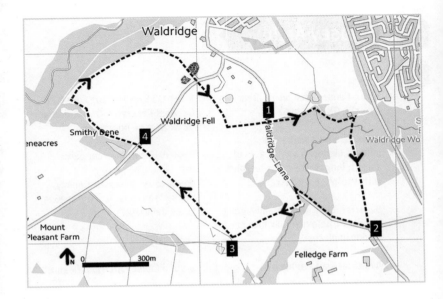

you reach a disused railway in an area of some old mine workings. Go right along this and follow it along the edge of a wood, with steeper ground to the right. Continue until a track leads off uphill on the right. Go right here and follow the track, keeping left when tracks join from the right to return to the car park.

Points of interest

Waldridge Fell is an extensive area of lowland heath (moorland less than 300m above sea level), and contains heather, bilberry and moorland grasses. These look stunning in late summer and autumn when the purple heather is in flower. Lowland heath is globally rare, which makes its careful management especially important. Coppicing of birch trees takes place on a rotational basis.

Causey Arch

START Causey Arch picnic area, NE6 5EJ, GR NZ205562

DISTANCE Short walk – 3½ miles/5.6km with 425ft/130m of ascent; long walk – 5½ miles/9km with 490ft/150m of ascent

SUMMARY Easy walks mainly along woodland/field tracks, which can be muddy in places

MAPS OS Explorer 307 Consett & Derwent Reservoir; OS Landranger 88 Newcastle upon Tyne

PARKING Picnic area car park

WHERE TO EAT AND DRINK Causey House Tearooms, T07813-673625 (open daily 9–4)

Two short walks along waymarked trails around Causey Arch and Beamish.

From the picnic area walk back out towards the entrance off the A6076, cross over and walk up past the pub. Go right at the junction and continue until you reach Coppy La. Go left along the lane, keeping left after houses into a wooded area, and continuing along the lane until you reach a metal gate at the edge of Coppy Woods. Keep on in the same direction through the woods and then between houses to reach a minor road behind Beamish Hall (**1**).

Turn right and walk along the road, until you reach the entrance of Beamish Burn picnic area. Turn left and walk through the car park to reach a footbridge over Beamish Burn; cross the bridge (**2**).

For the short walk, turn right here and follow the path through the woods to a road. Go left for a short distance until you come to a footpath marker on the right. Turn right along the track to emerge at the A6076. Turn right and walk along the path until you reach Causey Hall Farm, then cross the road and follow the path over Oxpasture Hill into Causey Gill. Cross the old railway line to reach a footbridge over the river (**6**).

Cross this and turn right, following the good path through the woods on what used to be the track bed of the old wagon way. Go up some wooden steps and turn right to reach Causey Arch. Don't cross this;

take the path on the left leading down steps to the river below – great views here of the bridge spanning the gorge. Follow the path alongside the stream, cross three footbridges, and at the fourth, turn right and climb the steps. At the top of the first section, go left onto a level track which you can follow back to the picnic area.

For the longer walk, at (2) go left and follow the path along the wall through dense yew trees until you reach a fence; turn right to reach a seat and cross a path. Turn left and enter Hellhole Woods, continuing along the path until a broad track starts to appear on the left. At the junction with this, go right and climb up through the trees to eventually reach an old railway line (3).

Go right and follow the track bed, passing through Shield Row, to reach a black ornate metal signpost (4). Turn right here and walk down past the houses and industrial units, keeping straight on through the wooded area and following signs for Tanfield Lea, to emerge onto a road. Turn right and walk along the path to the T-junction. Go left and walk a short distance up to the entrance to the now disused Tanfield Lea Railway (5). Cross the road and go through the entrance, keeping left beside a seat to enter the woods, then follow the path to reach a footbridge across Causey Burn (6) to join the shorter route which leads back to the car park.

15

16

Hamsterley Mill Woods

START Hamsterley Mill, NE39 1HE, GR NZ142560

DISTANCE Short walk – 4½ miles/7.2km with 525ft/160m of ascent; long walk – 6¼ miles/10km with 725ft/220m of ascent

SUMMARY Moderate walks mainly along woodland/field tracks, which can be muddy in places

MAPS OS Explorer 307 Consett & Derwent Reservoir; OS Landranger 88 Newcastle upon Tyne

PARKING Roadside parking area

WHERE TO EAT AND DRINK None

Two walks through the woods between Hamsterley Mill and Dipton.

From the car park cross the road and take the track leading off on the right. This will take you over the impressive Pontburn Viaduct. At the other side go right down some steps onto a track; don't go under the viaduct. Turn left and follow the track to the road. Turn right and walk a short distance to a footpath marker, leaving the road and taking the path through the woods. Cross Red Burn via the footbridge and continue uphill to reach a gate. Go through this into a field, following a path along the left side to reach Low Ewhurst Farm (1).

Keep left in front of the farm and follow the track to the T-junction. Turn right to shortly enter a field, going along the left side of this as far as a stile on the left. Cross it and follow the path through the woods, keeping left where it forks to exit the woods over a stile, and continue ahead over fields (2). At the second stile, go right alongside a hedge and into the woods. The path now contours across the hillside for about a mile (ignore any tracks leading off), through woods and gorse bushes, to reach a reedy tarn. Just after this cross a footbridge and turn right downhill alongside Pikewell Burn and follow the path to eventually reach a bridge over Pont Burn (3).

Cross the bridge and keep on the well-defined track through the woods. Pont Burn runs alongside to the right, and you cross it a couple of times

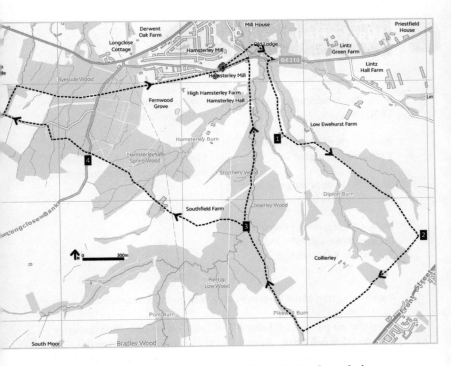

before reaching a footbridge with a ford to the right. Go through the gate and follow the track, keeping right where it meets the drive to Hamsterley Hall. At the road turn left and walk back along it to reach the car park.

For the longer walk, at (3) walk along the track as for the shorter route for a short distance until a track heads off uphill to the left. Take this and follow it through the woods, exiting into a field, then go diagonally left then right to reach a track. Turn left, go through the yard of Southfield Farm and go along the access track to the B6310 (4).

Go directly across into Black Byerside Woods, following the track downhill and keeping right at the junction to reach Cut Throat La. Turn left along the lane and continue as far as the entrance track to West Byerside Farm. Turn right along this to reach the Derwent Walk. Turn right onto the disused railway line and follow it back to the car park, crossing the B6310 along the way.

START Parkhead Station, DL13 2ES, GR NZ003432

DISTANCE 5¼ miles/8.4km with 330ft/100m of ascent

SUMMARY An easy walk mainly along disused railway lines

MAPS OS Explorer 307 Consett & Derwent Reservoir; OS Landranger 87 Hexham & Haltwhistle

PARKING Small parking area adjacent to the picnic area

WHERE TO EAT AND DRINK Parkhead Station, T01388-526434 www.parkheadstation.co.uk

A walk along part of the Waskerley Way, with great panoramic views.

From the car park go left behind Parkhead Station onto the Waskerley Way and through a gate. Now begins the long slow descent to the Hawksburn car park, which unfortunately means the return will be all uphill! There are great views down to the Waskerley Reservoir, which nestles in the valley down to your right. Keep following the old track bed until you reach a seat on the left (1).

Just beyond this a rough track crosses the railway. Turn right here and descend towards the reservoir, passing a house on the way. The Waskerley Reservoir is one of three in the area that supply nearby water treatment works, however their capacity isn't enough to meet demand so the Waskerley Reservoir can be gravity fed from the Burnhope Reservoir in Weardale if needed. Continue along the track until it forks beside a wall/gate (2).

Go left uphill along the access road and continue until the Hawksburn car park is reached (3). Leave the road, going left back onto the Waskerley Way. The Parkhead Station can be seen away in the distance, roughly about 2½ miles and 200ft of climbing. It's an easy walk all the way, passing through the Frosterley Cut, the only cutting on the route.

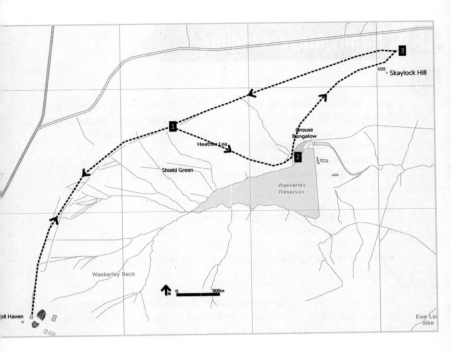

The rest of the old track bed has been built up on embankments over the boggy moorlands.

Points of interest

The Waskerley Way is a beautiful ten-mile route passing through a varied landscape: from urban fringe through to upland sheep farms, and then on to exposed heather moorland along part of the old Stanhope and Tyneside Railway.

18
19

Nanny Mayers Incline

START Whitehall picnic area, DH8 9AN, GR NZ077477

DISTANCE Short walk – 5 miles/8km with 530ft/160m of ascent; long walk – 8 miles/13km with 710ft/215m of ascent

SUMMARY An easy walk mainly along disused railway lines

MAPS OS Explorer 307 Consett & Derwent Reservoir; OS Landranger 87 Hexham & Haltwhistle

PARKING Small parking area adjacent to the picnic area

WHERE TO EAT AND DRINK None

A walk along some of the disused railway lines in north-west County Durham.

Leave the car park via the picnic area at its west end, and join the disused railway line first west and then south through a series of cuttings. This is the Waskerley Way path, which follows the track bed of the Stanhope to Consett railway. It will be followed as far as the farm at Red House, but make note of the seat at the corner of a wood (1), which will be where you will return to later in the walk.

Keep on the track bed until you reach Red House (2), then go right, heading across a field. At the other side re-join the track bed and go right towards Waskerley Station (3).

For the shorter walk, at the station go right through a gate into a yard and pass some of the old railway buildings to the top of Nanny Mayer's Incline. This is well defined as it descends into the valley bottom. At the bottom go through a gate and keep alongside the wall on the right until you come to a white metal gate (4). The conditions underfoot deteriorate, so leave the old railway line at the gate and go diagonally right up across the fields to reach a gate and re-join the outward route (1). Turn left and walk back along the Waskerley Way to the car park.

For the longer route, at (3) keep on the railway line and pass the buildings, then go through a gate and onto open moorland. Continue

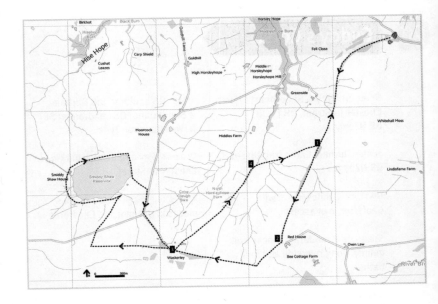

until a track goes off on the right. Go right here to reach the road,
crossing and continuing in the same direction over the heather
moorlands towards Smiddy Shaw Reservoir. On reaching a track
junction, go left and follow the track around the reservoir towards
Smiddy Shaw House. Go over a footbridge and pass through the yard
of the house and then onto the dam wall. Continue along the dam to
the corner, turn right and continue to a car park. Keep left and follow a
track to reach the road again, where you turn right and follow this to the
entrance to Waskerley Farm. Go left and follow the track to the car park
at the station (3).

Points of interest

Waskerley Farm was once at the junction of two railways, the
Crook to Waskerley and the Stanhope to Consett. The station had
sidings, a shed for six engines and wagon repair shops. There was
also a village for the families of the railway workers, a church, a chapel, a
school and shops, all at 1,150ft above sea level.

Cuddy's Corse

START St Mary & St Cuthbert Church, Chester-le-Street, DH3 3QB, GR NZ275513

FINISH Durham Cathedral, DH1 3EH, GR NZ273421

DISTANCE 8 miles/13km with 620ft/190m of ascent

SUMMARY A moderate, linear walk mainly along riverside and field paths

MAPS OS Explorer 308 Durham & Sunderland; OS Landranger 88 Newcastle upon Tyne

PARKING Pay and display parking in Chester-le-Street

WHERE TO EAT AND DRINK Various places in Durham and Chester-le-Street

An interesting walk between Chester-le-Street and Durham, partly along the banks of the River Wear.

From the church go right along Church Chare to the mini roundabout. Go left here along the footpath beside the school to reach Roman Av. Continue along this and cross the A167 at the end to reach the Riverside Park. Cross the park and go right along the riverside path as far as Lumley Bridge (1).

Leave the park, cross left over the bridge and then go left into the golf course, keeping left to rejoin the riverside path again. Follow this along the river, and then over fields to reach Great Lumley (2). Go right along the road, and then right into Cambridge Dr, following this to Exeter Cl. Go left onto the bridleway, and follow this over fields to Cocken La. Go right and walk along this to a road junction (3).

Go left and walk along the road to a footpath on the right, which leads down through woods. At the bottom cross over the River Wear via the footbridge to reach Finchale Priory, passing in front of this and keeping along the road to a junction opposite Frankland Prison. Go right along the road, then take the footpath on the left beside some houses. Follow the lane around the walls of the prison, cross a disused railway line and continue along Frankland La, passing Frankland Farm to reach a road beside Crook Hall (4).

Go right along the road and follow it beside the River Wear to reach the Framwellgate Bridge. Go under this and then right up the steps to go right over the bridge and follow the road up into Durham Market Place. From here go right up Saddler St towards the Palace Green, keeping right along Owengate to the green opposite the cathedral.

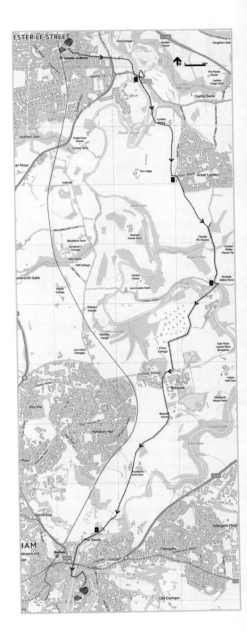

Burnhope Burn

START St Edmund's Church, Edmundbyers, DH8 9NQ, GR NZ014501

DISTANCE 8 miles/13km with 820ft/250m of ascent

SUMMARY A moderate walk over rolling heather moors, generally on good tracks

MAPS OS Explorer 307 Consett & Derwent Reservoir; OS Landranger 87 Hexham & Haltwhistle

PARKING Roadside parking outside the church

WHERE TO EAT AND DRINK The Punchbowl Inn, Edmundbyers, T01207-255545, http://thepunchbowlinn.info

A walk over Edmundbyers Common, with solitude and magnificent views.

From the church, go downhill along the road to the junction with the B6278. Turn right and follow the road out of the village. At the sharp left bend, leave the road and take the track on the right going through a gate, and then keep left where the track splits, following the wall. Stay on this track until it meets the stream in Swan Dale (**1**).

Cross the stream and climb right up past the ruined buildings to reach the corner of a wall. The path levels out here. Go left and follow the track alongside the wall, then over open moorland and pastures heading for Pedam's Oak, which can be seen clearly in the distance. When you reach the farm go through the gates and pass to the left of the barn into the yard. The ruins are very impressive, but also dangerously unstable (**2**).

Leave the yard by the double gates in the left corner and follow the track over the open moorlands – great views over the Burnhope Burn valley – over several more rough pastures to reach another ruined building at Belmount. Go over the stile and continue along the track behind the buildings until you reach a fence. Turn right and go along the path

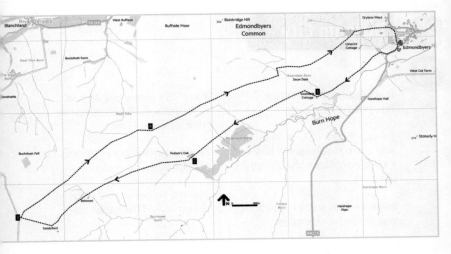

to another gate with a boundary stone beside it; go through this and continue ahead to reach a road (**3**).

Take the track heading diagonally right away from the road over the moors, and stay on this until you come to a small cairn on the right. Leave the track and follow the narrow path through the heather until you reach a gate in a wall. Go through the gate and keep right along the track over the moors to another gate. Follow the path across the enclosed pasture. A short detour off to your left reveals Cuthbert's Currick, a cairn which gives great views over the border into Northumberland and the village of Blanchland (**4**).

Exit the enclosure via a gate. Stay on the track over the moorlands, cross a stream at Swandale Head, and then keep right alongside a walled enclosure to reach the ford across Black Burn. Ford the stream and continue along the track to reach the B6306, turn right downhill and then turn right at the junction into the lane leading down to the church.

Durham City

START Durham Market Place, DH1 3PN, GR NZ274425

DISTANCE Short walk – 2 miles/3.2km with 225ft/70m of ascent; long walk – 4¾ miles/7.6km with 610ft/185m of ascent

SUMMARY Easy walks mainly along woodland/riverside paths

MAPS OS Explorer 308 Durham & Sunderland; OS Landranger 88 Newcastle upon Tyne

PARKING Various pay and display car parks in Durham

WHERE TO EAT AND DRINK Various outlets around the market place

Two short walks around Durham City along the banks of the River Wear.

From the market place go right down Silver St, cross over Framwellgate Bridge and go down the steps on the left at the far side; at the bottom of these go right along the riverside path. There are great views of the cathedral from here. Continue along to Prebends Bridge; don't cross it, but continue along the river until the path leads up some steps to St Oswald's church (**1**). Go right through the churchyard to reach Church St, turn left and walk along the road towards the Students Union building (**4**).

Immediately before this, turn left and cross back over the River Wear via Kingsgate Bridge, and go down the steep steps on the left at the other side. Once on the riverside path go right and follow this to reach Prebends Bridge again. Turn right uphill onto South Bailey, following this until the cathedral is reached, and turn left along Dun Cow La into the Palace Green. After exploring the buildings around the green, leave via Owengate, going down to join Saddler St and turning left back to the market place.

For the longer walk, at (**1**) go across Church St and take the alleyway alongside the school, which will bring you out onto the A177 opposite the Palatine Centre. Cross the road and go straight ahead alongside the university buildings, keeping left going past Mountjoy House and then into Great High Wood. Follow the path along the top of the wood until you reach a gate (2). Just before the gate a path goes left downhill; take this and at the bottom turn left, following the path until you come to the A177 (3).

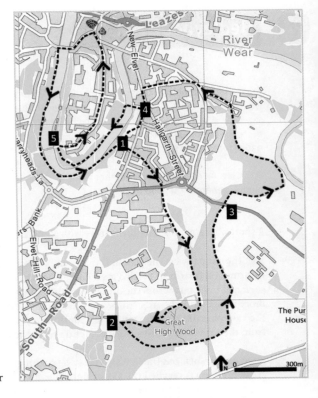

Cross the road and go through the kissing gate, following the path around Maiden Castle. At the end keep left onto the riverside path as far as the sports ground. Go left and walk around the pitches to enter some buildings. Go left through these along the road to Whinney Hill, cross this and go right and then left passing in front of the Law Courts. Keep on in the same direction along Court La to reach New Elvet, turn right and walk along to the Students Union building (4). Continue the route following the shorter walk from (4).

Points of interest

Time should be allowed to explore the historic buildings around the Palace Green: Bishop Cosin's Hall and the Library, the University Library, Abbey House, the Almshouses, the castle and of course the cathedral.

Hedleyhope Fell

START Hedleyhope Fell, DL13 4PR,
GR NZ149414

DISTANCE 2¼ miles/3.6km with
330ft/100m of ascent

SUMMARY An easy walk over heather
moors, generally on good tracks

MAPS OS Explorer 307 Consett &
Derwent Reservoir; OS Landranger
88 Newcastle upon Tyne

PARKING Nature reserve car park

WHERE TO EAT AND DRINK None

A short walk around the nature reserve with grand views.

Exit the car park via the gate in the corner, passing a couple of
information boards to reach a gate. Go through this and follow the
surfaced track out across the moor, shortly to reach a viewpoint with
more information boards. There are good views of the whole walk and
the valley/nature reserve from here. Continue in the same direction
from the viewpoint until a track comes up from the right (**1**).

Keep on the surfaced track; it's an easy walk with great views until a
cross-junction is reached (**2**). Go straight ahead and follow the track as
it makes a loop around the moors to return to the cross-junction (**2**). Go
straight ahead downhill now, steep in places and it can also be a bit wet
underfoot. Take the first track on the right and follow back along the
valley as far as a small pond down to your left (**3**).

Go right uphill along a good track and keep right where it splits and
then right again at the cairn and then keep straight on. It's a bit of a pull
up, but soon you will reach the surfaced track at the top (**1**). Turn left
and follow this back to the car park, passing the information boards/
viewpoint again.

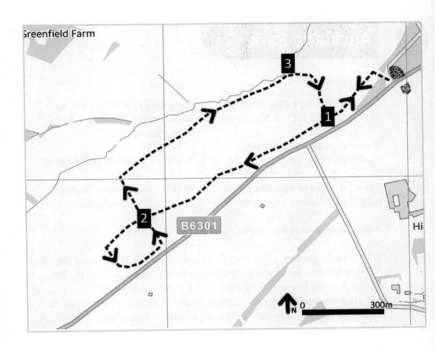

Greenfield Farm

3

1

2

B6301

Hi

N 0   300m

Points of interest

Hedleyhope Fell is a nature reserve to the north-east of Tow Law, County Durham. The reserve, which is managed by Durham Wildlife Trust, consists of some 200 acres of mainly mid-altitude heathland.

Auckland Park

START Castle Chare car park, Bishop Auckland, DL14 7JF, GR NZ212299

DISTANCE 3¼ miles/5.2km with 430ft/130m of ascent

SUMMARY An easy walk along field paths and a disused railway track

MAPS OS Explorer 305 Bishop Auckland; OS Landranger 93 Middlesbrough

PARKING Pay and display parking

WHERE TO EAT AND DRINK Various places in Bishop Auckland

A short walk around Bishop Auckland and the deer park.

From the car park go right along Kingsway and then right onto Durham Rd. Continue as far as the footpath sign next to the house on the left. Go left here up the steps and then over a stile into the field, cross this and then go right along the park/golf course boundary wall. Continue following this over several fields until a stile gives access onto a disused railway line at Coundongate (1).

Turn left here and walk along the old track bed of the former Brandon to Bishop Auckland railway. Keep on this until two bridges over the track are reached; go under the first and then take the path on the right, which will take you up to the top of the second bridge. Go right over the bridge and then through a gate into a field. Walk downhill along the left edge of this field and the one after to reach a gate (2).

Go through the gate and into Auckland Park, keeping left onto a track that continues through Hazel Bank Plantation, which will eventually bring you to a footbridge over Coundon Beck (3). Cross the footbridge and then go left uphill alongside the River Gaunless; at the top of the climb the imposing Deer Shelter appears. Keep to the right of this and then right at the next junction to reach the walls around the castle. Go left along these to a gate, go through it and pass in front of the gates and then through the entrance gates into the market place. Go left along Castle Chare and then right onto Kingsway to return to the car park.

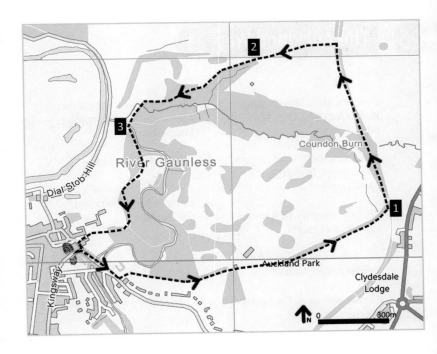

Points of interest

Auckland Castle, also known locally as the Bishop's Palace, was originally owned by the Church of England for the Prince Bishops of Durham for more than 800 years. Auckland Castle was originally established as a hunting lodge. The principal seat of the Bishops of Durham from 1832, it was transferred in July 2012 to the Auckland Castle Trust, a charitable foundation, to restore both the castle and grounds and also establish permanent exhibitions on the history of Christianity in Britain and the North-east.

The Auckland Way

START Auckland Way car park, Bishop Auckland, DL14 8QW, GR NZ221291

FINISH Whitworth Road car park, Spennymoor, DL16 7QS, GR NZ245337

DISTANCE 3¾ miles/6km with 220ft/65m of ascent

SUMMARY An easy walk along disused railway tracks

MAPS OS Explorer 305 Bishop Auckland; OS Landranger 93 Middlesbrough

PARKING Free car park

WHERE TO EAT AND DRINK Various places in Bishop Auckland/ Spennymoor

A linear walk along The Auckland Way between Bishop Auckland and Spennymoor.

Exit the car park towards the roundabout on the A688 and go left up the path onto the disused railway line, which is now called The Auckland Way. It climbs gently uphill as it passes between houses. Go through a tunnel and continue to the car park at Coundongate. Pass the old station building and continue along the track bed, passing Auckland Park/golf course on your left. This section of the track is elevated and gives fine views over the surrounding countryside. Head into a cutting to reach a set of double bridges over the line (1).

Continue north along the track bed to the village of Binchester. The original village was a Roman military station on Dere St, to the east of here. It was called Vinovia, which means 'pleasant place'. Cross Long La, then go downhill to pass under a steel bridge over the line. Just beyond this are the remains of the platform from the old Byres Green Station, now a picnic area (2). The name 'Byres' means 'ancient woods'; at one time the nearby village was surrounded by them.

The track bed drops to cross another minor road, then climbs and makes a long right turn to pass behind some houses at Bishop Close. Continue along another elevated section of track, again offering great views, to reach the car park at the Whitworth Road.

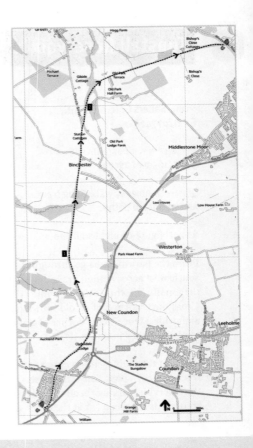

Points of interest

Now disused, the railway line ran from Spennymoor to Bishop Auckland and was built in two stages. In 1841 the section between Byres Green and Spennymoor was opened as part of the Clarence Railway Company Byres Green Railway, which served Port Clarence on Teesside. Then in 1885 the NER opened the line between Byres Green and Bishop Auckland, for passengers. The complete line formed a link between Bishop Auckland and Cornforth, connecting the Darlington to Bishop Auckland line with the East Coast mainline. The route was closed in 1939.

Tunstall Reservoir

START Salters Gate, DL13 4JN, GR NZ077426

DISTANCE 3¾ miles/6km with 550ft/165m of ascent

SUMMARY An easy walk along tracks and woodland paths

MAPS OS Explorer 307 Consett & Derwent Reservoir; OS Landranger 87 Hexham & Haltwhistle

PARKING Roadside parking

WHERE TO EAT AND DRINK None

A short figure-of-eight walk around the Tunstall Reservoir.

From the parking area go through the gate in the stone wall and go south-west across rough grass. Ignore the well-defined track going diagonally left; this is the way you will return at the end of the walk. Cross the track bed of an old railway line and continue downhill alongside a fence to the corner of a wood. Go left downhill alongside this to reach a track junction (**1**).

Go right through a gate, keeping on the track as it crosses the top of the reservoir, then past Tunstall House. Continue along the road around the reservoir, passing through a parking area to reach the dam. Go left across this and keep left at the other side to pass between stone gate posts (**2**).

Leave the road and follow the path through Backstone Bank Woods; at the end of the woods cross a stile onto a track (**1**). Turn right and follow the track uphill between the trees; the track bears to the left as it passes by a black barn. At the top of the climb keep left at the track junction to re-cross the old railway line, and continue straight ahead to return to the parking area at Salters Gate.

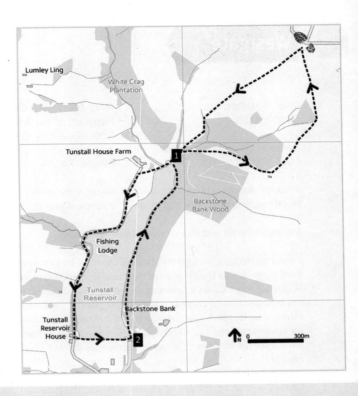

Points of interest

Tunstall Reservoir was constructed in 1879 to supply drinking water for Willington, Shildon, Sedgefield and Spennymoor. When the valley was flooded, three houses and many acres of farm and woodland were drowned.

The now disused line was built by the Stockton and Darlington Railway Company in 1845 to link the New Derwent Iron Company works at Consett with Crook.

Quarry Wood is the haunt of foxes and roe deer. There is still evidence of quarrying but spoil heaps were planted with larch trees many years ago, an early example of land reclamation.

Westgate

START Westgate, DL13 1LN,
GR NY904380

DISTANCE 4½ miles/7.2km with
650ft/195m of ascent

SUMMARY A moderate walk along
moorland/riverside paths and roads

MAPS OS Explorer OL31 North
Pennines; OS Landranger 92
Barnard Castle & Richmond

PARKING Roadside parking

WHERE TO EAT AND DRINK The Hare &
Hounds, Westgate, T01388-517212

A delightful walk with fine views of Upper Weardale.

From the parking area go right along the road and cross left over a
footbridge across the river after the campsite. Then go right onto the
Weardale Way. Cross a field and go left between houses. At the end of
the lane go right to cross a footbridge, regaining the riverbank, and
follow it upstream to the Daddryshield Bridge. Cross the A688 and keep
on upstream along the riverbank until you reach a footpath sign on the
left. Leave the river here, going left across the field to reach the road
again (1).

Cross the road, turn right up the track beside the houses, then left
into the field in front of the next house, and then right over a stile,
continuing across fields to a farm. Enter the yard and go left between
the house/garage and keep straight on through another yard, passing
stables, to exit through double metal gates into a field. At the far side of
the field cross a bridge, crossing the field beyond to a gate on the left of
the house. Here, join a track and go left, then almost immediately right
uphill. Where the track turns sharp right, go through a gate into a rough
pasture, crossing this diagonally left towards Glenwhelt. At the barn
turn left to a gate, which leads to a road in front of the farm (2).

Take the footpath on the left of the road, crossing another rough pasture
and aiming for a small group of trees which comes into view. Pass to the
right of these and continue downhill to ford a stream beside a wall. After
crossing the stream, keep alongside the wall as it climbs uphill, passing
ruined farms to reach a gate (3).

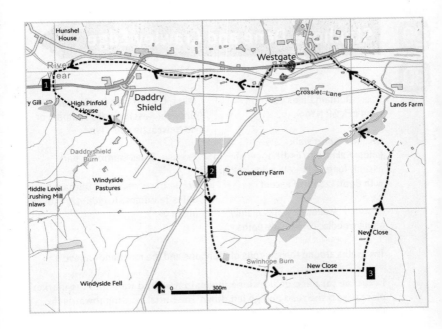

Go through the gate and then turn left onto a track leading downhill. Keep on this to Swinhopeburn. Here, turn right to reach a minor road, then left along the road where it forks, keeping right to head back into Westgate village. At the Hare and Hounds pub go left along the A688 to get back to the start.

Points of interest

Westgate village consists of two main parts: High Westgate, which is the older, and Westgate Village. At High Westgate a small castle or hunting lodge was built by the Prince Bishops of Durham during their grand visits into Weardale – forerunners of the present-day trippers perhaps, who come into the Dale still searching for wildlife, though hopefully for a different reason!

Stanhope Dene and Crawley Edge

START Durham Dales Centre, DL13 2FJ, GR NY995392

DISTANCE Short walk – 4½ miles/7.2km with 650ft/195m of ascent; long walk – 6¼ miles/10km with 800ft/240m of ascent

SUMMARY Moderate walks mainly along woodland/riverside paths

MAPS OS Explorer 307 Consett & Derwent Reservoir; OS Landranger 88 Newcastle upon Tyne

PARKING Dales Centre car park

WHERE TO EAT AND DRINK Durham Dales Tearooms, T01388-527650 (open 9–4)

Two walks around the environs of Stanhope and the moorlands above it.

Leave the car park, go left along the main road and walk into the market place. Cross the road and go left down The Butts, heading towards the river. At the bottom of the road, turn right onto the riverside path, which leads upstream to the Stanhope Swimming Pool. Turn right past the pool to the main road, go left for a short distance, then turn right along a track in front of Stanhope Hall. Follow this as far as the footbridge across the river **(1)**.

Don't cross this; keep on the west side of the stream and follow the path, initially fenced along field edges and then into the woods. Continue through the woods until you reach another footbridge, cross this and climb the steep steps to join a wide track. Go left along this through old quarries to reach derelict mine buildings **(2)**.

Just after passing a large single-storey building on the right, take the track going off uphill on the right, following a wall through gorse bushes to reach a gate. Go right along the track, and follow it through Heathery Burn to reach a road. Go directly across the road to reach an old mine track, turning right and following this downhill. At the buildings go left and then leave the track, following a grassy track on the right alongside the wall/fence to reach a gate. Go left along a path through the heather onto Crawleyside Edge, and continue until you reach a fork in the path **(3)**.

Go right downhill to reach a double set of kissing gates. Go through both of these and then diagonally left to join a fence alongside the quarry. Follow this until it turns sharp right. Go down over footbridges and then past houses to reach a road. Turn right and walk along to the first road on the left, go down this to the main road, and turn left again to reach the Dales Centre.

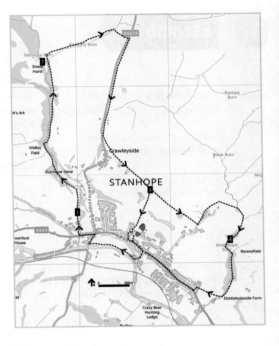

For the longer walk, keep straight on at point (3) along Crawleyside Edge to reach a road. Turn left uphill to a farm, go left through a gate and then keep right to pass behind the farm. Ford the stream and follow it right, downstream. As you reach the woods, cross the stream again and follow the path to reach a footbridge (4). Cross the bridge and go right downstream, following the path through the woods until the next bridge across the stream. Cross this, then cross the stile into a field, keeping right alongside the wall to a lane between houses. Go along this, then turn left along Woodcroft Gdns to the main road. Turn right and follow this back through Stanhope to the Dales Centre.

Points of interest

The Stanhope Fossil Tree grew in a forest of the Mid-Carboniferous period (about 250 million years ago) near Edmundbyers Cross, now 1,550ft above sea level. As its vegetable matter decayed this was replaced by sand, which has formed a perfect cast in hard ganister. The tree was brought to Stanhope and erected here in 1962 by Mr J. G. Beaston.

START Bondgate car park, Bishop Auckland, DL14 7PG, GR NZ209301

DISTANCE 3¾ miles/6km with 220ft/65m of ascent

SUMMARY An easy walk along fields and riverbanks; can be muddy in places

MAPS OS Explorer 305 Bishop Auckland; OS Landranger 93 Middlesbrough

PARKING Pay and display car parking

WHERE TO EAT AND DRINK Various places in Bishop Auckland

A short walk from Bishop Auckland to the Saxon church at Escomb.

From the car park turn right along North Bondgate, cross the A689 at the roundabout, go left into West Rd and then right onto Hexham St. At the end, go down steps to emerge at the West Mill picnic area (1).

Go left along the road between allotments and the rugby ground, and at the end of the road cross a stile into a field. Cross the field, keeping right into scrub trees and gorse bushes alongside the river. This path can be very wet and muddy in places. Keep right along the riverbank to reach a footbridge across a stream. Staying by the riverside, cross several pastures to reach the end of a lane. Go left along this into Escomb village and the church (2).

Leave the village along Bede Cl, cross two stiles and then go right. Stay along the edge of the fields to cross a railway line via a bridge, then continue across fields in the same direction to join Green La. Go left through fields behind houses to a terrace of cottages called Primrose Villas, AD1874 (3).

Go left down the lane and re-cross the railway, cross a stile to enter a field, then go diagonally right downhill to re-join the outward route as far as the picnic area (1).

Stay on the lane until it reaches the road, turn left and follow it to the old Newton Cap Bridge over the River Wear. Don't cross this; go right along

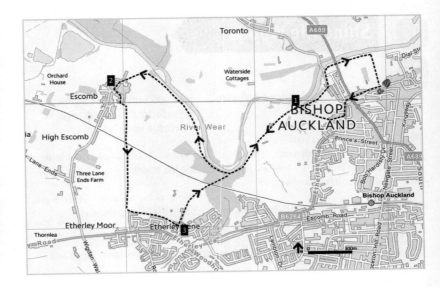

the riverside path, under the new Newton Cap Viaduct, until a footpath on the right leads you uphill back into Bondgate and the car park.

Points of interest

Escomb's church is the oldest complete Saxon church in England, and one of the best examples of Anglo-Saxon architecture in Western Europe. It was built in the second half of the seventh century with stone taken from the Roman fort of Binchester.

Shincliffe Woods

Start Sunderland Bridge, DH1 3SP, GR NZ264377

Distance Short walk – 4¾ miles/7.6km with 320ft/100m of ascent; long walk – 7 miles/11.3km with 620ft/190m of ascent

Summary Easy walks mainly along woodland/riverside paths

Maps OS Explorer 308 Durham & Sunderland; OS Landranger 88 Newcastle upon Tyne

Parking Roadside parking beside the old bridge

Where to eat and drink Seven Stars, Shincliffe, T0191-384-8454

Two walks around the fields and woods between Sunderland Bridge and Shincliffe.

From the old bridge go left through an arched gateway and then under the A167. Continue along the road to a fork and go left uphill, the road doubling back to the right to reach an old medieval church. Go left beyond this into a yard area in front of an imposing open barn (**1**).

Go right here to pass a cottage, then the track turns left and continues straight ahead over parklands. Stay on this, passing High Croxdale Farm. The way then becomes a grassy track along field edges, reaching a track running through woodlands. Go left along this, crossing fields to reach a broad vehicle track (**2**). Turn left onto the track and follow across more fields to High Butterby Farm (**4**).

Go left in front of the farmhouse onto a track, which runs between fields on your left and woods on the right. Follow this past Croxdale Wood House to eventually enter the farmyard behind the old church again (**1**). Go right to pass the church and retrace your outward route back to the start.

For the longer walk, at (2) cross the broad track and go through a gate onto Strawberry La, following this to reach the access road to West Grange Farm. Go right along this to the A177. Cross the road and go left along the footpath to Shincliffe village (**3**).

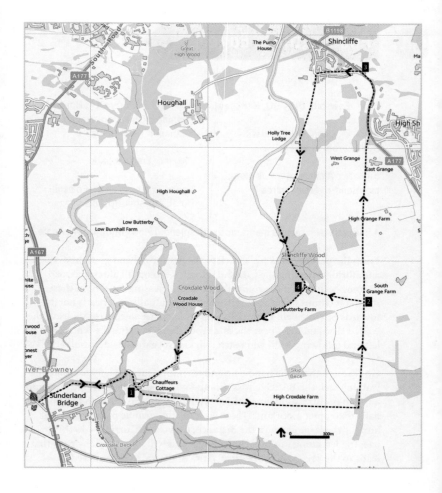

Re-cross the road and pass the Seven Stars pub to enter the village. Keep on through the houses, and at the bottom of the road go left onto Hall La, pass the garden centre and continue as far as Shincliffe Hall. Here, keep left on the path leading into the woods, staying on this to reach the banks of the River Wear. Go left upstream; the path will leave the riverbank and climb steeply up through the trees to High Butterby Farm. Go up the steps to join the track in front of the house **(4)**.

Puddingthorn Edge

START Cowshill, DL13 1JQ, NY855406

DISTANCE 5¼ miles/8.4km with 890ft/270m of ascent

SUMMARY A moderate walk along moorland/riverside paths

MAPS OS Explorer OL31 North Pennines; OS Landranger 87 Hexham & Haltwhistle

PARKING Free car park

WHERE TO EAT AND DRINK Cowshill Hotel, Cowshill, T01388-537236

A fine walk over remote moorlands with splendid views of Upper Weardale.

From the parking area walk back to the main road and go right over a footbridge, passing the Cowshill Hotel. Keep uphill along the road to some cottages on the right. Take the lane passing in front of these. At first it climbs fairly steeply, then more gradually as it heads north towards Burtree Fell. Eventually you will reach a gate; here you leave the walled lane and head over the open moorland, keeping the fence on your left and following it till you reach two kissing gates beside a wall (1).

Go through the right-hand gate and then immediately left alongside the wall to reach the B6295. Cross this and go through the gate opposite into a rough pasture, following the left wall to a gate. Go through the gate back onto open moorland. There isn't any discernible path at first, but aim for the large cairn in the distance, Clevison's Currick – do this by keeping left along Puddingthorn Edge. You will join a sketchy path that leads to the cairn; there are great views of the valley from here (2).

From the cairn follow the path steeply downhill, aiming for an old wooden shed beside a wall/gate. Go through the gate into a walled lane, which leads downhill to the A688 beside an old chapel, now converted into a house. Go right along the road to the track leading to Burnt Hills at Lanehead (3).

Go left down this, then left again by the house, crossing fields and a stream to reach Heathery Bridge. Go left uphill across rough pasture and keep left to cross more rough pastures to Low Allers. Join a track here, which will take you downstream along the banks of the river, passing old quarries to Burtreeford Bridge. Go through a gate onto a road. Turn left over the bridge and then right between the houses of Burtreeford, keeping along the road which will eventually bring you out onto the A688 in Cowshill. Turn left and walk the short distance back to the car park.

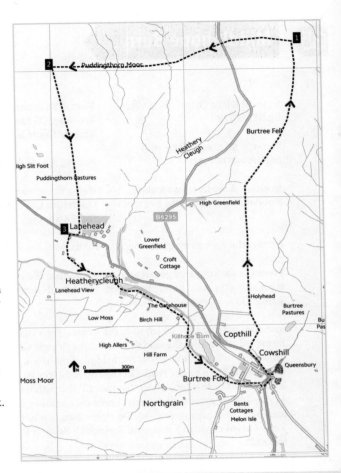

The area around Cowshill was heavily mined for lead in years gone by, and the remains of mining activity still scar the landscape hundreds of years later. The Killihope Mining Museum, located a few miles along the valley, gives a good insight into life in the area during the mining era.

35 Middlehope Burn

START St John's Chapel, DL13 1QF, GR NY886378

DISTANCE 5½ miles/8.8km with 640ft/195m of ascent

SUMMARY A moderate walk along moorland/riverside paths and roads

MAPS OS Explorer OL31 North Pennines; OS Landranger 92 Barnard Castle & Richmond

PARKING Roadside parking

WHERE TO EAT AND DRINK The Chatterbox Café, St John's Chapel, To1388-537536

A delightful walk along quiet lanes and woods, with fine views.

From the parking area go left along the road into the village, then turn right along the road beside the green, which leads down to the village school (**1**).

Just after passing this, go left over the stream, then right through a farmyard and across the field to Ponderlane Bridge. Cross this and follow the path straight across the field to climb steps, and then across another field to a minor road. Go slightly right to a farm track on the left, and follow this for a short distance till the path leads off left through a fallen-down stone wall. It then climbs over fields to reach a stile, leading to another minor road. Go right along this to the end, at Slit Vein. Go left through a gate onto Seeingsike Rd, and follow this until it forks (**2**).

Here, go right steeply downhill along the badly eroded track, crossing the stream at the bottom, then turn right and follow the stream. It's wet and boggy in places, but it improves as you head down the valley. Pass the remains of old mine buildings and keep on downstream. The valley is more heavily wooded now and you will also pass a number of fine little waterfalls, the most impressive of which is just before reaching a cottage. Pass to the right of the cottage onto a lane, which takes you into Westgate village. Keep right along this to reach the A688 (**3**).

Go right along the main road and go left over a footbridge across the

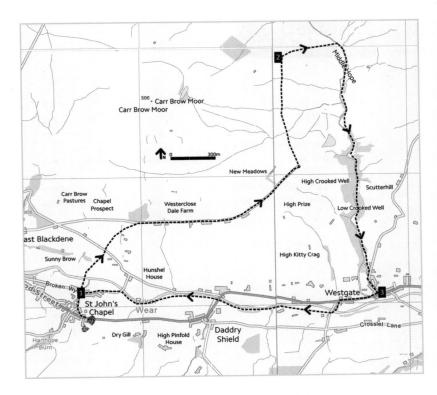

river after the campsite. Then turn right onto the Weardale Way, cross a field and go left between houses. At the end of the lane go right to cross a footbridge, regaining the riverbank, which you follow upstream to the Daddryshield Bridge. Cross the A688 and keep on upstream along the riverbank until you see a footbridge and stepping stones across the river. Go left along the lane to reach the school again (1). Turn left along the lane back to the start.

Points of interest

Slitts Woods, Westgate, is notable for its waterfalls, natural beauty, wildlife and industrial past.

Frosterley

START Durham Dales Centre,
DL13 2FJ, GR NY995392

DISTANCE 6 miles/9.7km with
780ft/235m of ascent

SUMMARY A moderate walk mainly
along moorland paths and country
lanes

MAPS OS Explorer 307 Consett &
Derwent Reservoir; OS Landranger
88 Newcastle upon Tyne

PARKING Dales Centre car park

WHERE TO EAT AND DRINK Durham
Dales Tearooms, To1388-527650
(open 9–4)

A walk over the moors to Frosterley, returning alongside the Weardale
Railway.

From the car park at the Dales Centre, turn left along the A688 and walk
through Stanhope village, passing the church and fossil tree on your left.
Keep on until you reach the garage at the east end of the village, then
turn left into Woodcroft Gdns, taking the footpath on the right between
houses to enter a field. Go along the left edge of the field, exit through a
gate and descend to cross a footbridge over Shittlehope Burn. Go up the
steep bank directly ahead through the hawthorn bushes, going slightly
left, to reach a track. Go left along this, and through a gate, then keep
along the track as it climbs towards the farm ahead. Enter the yard and
go left behind the house, aiming for a gate in the wall that gives access to
a slanting track, which takes you out onto the open moors (**1**).

At the top of the track go right along a grassy track over the moors –
great views here over Upper Weardale. On reaching a gate in a wire
fence, don't go through it; turn left and follow the fence to the next gate.
Here, go left along a grassy track away from the fence, climbing slightly
to a wall/fence, cross this and then aim diagonally across the rough
pasture, heading towards the ruins of an old cottage in the distance.
Cross the fence in front of the cottage, and then go right over a stile into
the next field, going right alongside the wall to another stile in the facing
wall. Cross this and continue downhill to join a rough track beside the
farm. Go left along this through a couple of pastures to reach Intake La.
Turn right and walk down the lane to the A689 (**2**).

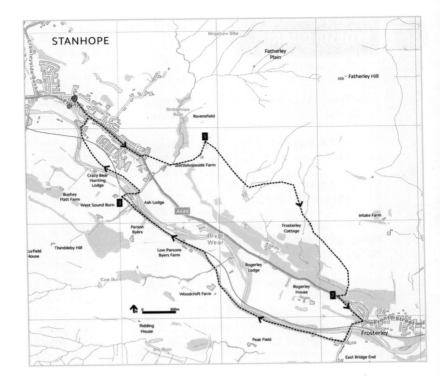

Go left along the main road towards Frosterley village. Don't go into the village, however; take the first junction on the right heading towards the Wear Valley railway station. Cross the bridges over the river/railway, then go right at the next road junction. This lane leads back towards Stanhope, at first running next to the River Wear, and later alongside the railway tracks. Walk as far as the entrance to a caravan park (3).

Turn right and follow the road, first over the railway and then over the River Wear. Just after crossing the river, take the footpath on the left through the fields to Stanhope. Continue, passing under the railway line twice more before reaching some houses. Turn right and walk along The Butts, which will bring you out into the market place in Stanhope. Go left along the road back to the car park.

Wolsingham

START Wolsingham, DL13 3DG, GR NZ075375

DISTANCE 6 miles/9.7km with 870ft/265m of ascent

SUMMARY A moderate walk mainly along field and moorland paths

MAPS OS Explorer OL31 North Pennines; OS Landranger 92 Barnard Castle & Richmond

PARKING Demesne Mill picnic area car park

WHERE TO EAT AND DRINK The Black Bull, Wolsingham, T01388-527332, www.blackbullwolsingham.co.uk

A walk around the Tunstall valley, from the valley bottom to the moors above.

Leave the car park through the gate in the northwest corner, and follow the path running alongside Waskerley Beck. Where this turns sharp left, go through the kissing gate and cross the meadow to an old mill race. Cross this and go through another kissing gate, then go right to cross a footbridge, keeping right past a seat to reach a gate. Go through this and then go left alongside the hedge uphill to a road. Cross this and take the footpath behind the seat, on the right of some gates. Walk uphill alongside the wall/fence through several pastures to reach the ruins of Park Wall farm. Here, cross the wall via a tall ladder stile (1).

Go right to twin metal gates – great views here across Weardale to the distant Cleveland Hills. Go through the left gate and follow the track, initially along the edge of a wood, then along field edges to pass Jofless Cottage. Continue along the track to High Jofless Farm, going left through the yard and passing the buildings, then at the gate beyond turn left and follow the path across the fields. Exit onto the road near the dam of Tunstall Reservoir, go right across the dam and follow the road as it climbs steeply to a farm (2).

At the farm go right along a level track heading south towards a wooded area, and pass alongside this to enter another wooded area where a stream is crossed. Go left uphill on a slippery stony path to exit the woods and then follow a broad track along the edge of the moors. Keep on this until you reach a fork; go right downhill towards Baal Hill House farm (3).

Pass to the left of the large barns and go through the gates, then continue diagonally left down across the field. Pass through some trees and keep on downhill along the left edge of the field. At the bottom, exit onto a lane, turn right along this for a short distance, then go left at a footpath sign. Follow the path across fields to reach some cottages, go through the gate and go straight ahead between them onto the B6296. Turn right and walk back to the picnic area.

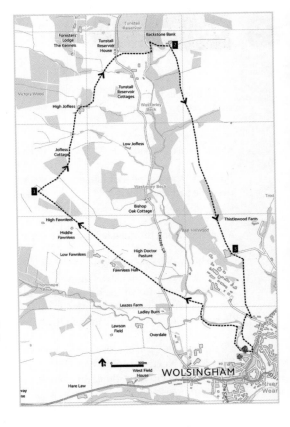

Points of interest

Backstone Bank Wood and Baal Hill Woods are Sites of Special Scientific Interest in the Wear valley. The area once formed part of a much larger expanse owned by the Prince Bishops of Durham from the late thirteenth century, protected both for its deer and its timber.

Rookhope

Start Rookhope, DL13 2BG,
GR NY938429

Distance 6½ miles/10.5km with
690ft/210m of ascent

Summary A moderate walk along
riverside paths and roads

Maps OS Explorer OL31 North
Pennines; OS Landranger 87
Hexham & Haltwhistle

Parking Roadside parking

Where to eat and drink The
Rookhope Inn, Rookhope,
T01388-517215

A fine walk along the quiet lanes and woods of the Rookhope valley.

From the Rookhope Inn cross over the bridge and go left down the lane towards some industrial units, going left to pass in front of them. Continue on the broad track through areas of spoil heaps, remnants of the area's former mining activities. Climb past Smailsburn Farm, and then alongside a conifer plantation to a gate (1).

Go through the gate to join a rough track, turn left and follow this downhill to North Hanging Wells Farm, passing through the yard onto the road. Go right along this for a short distance until you reach a footpath marker on the left. Go through the gate and follow the path down to the banks of Rookhope Burn. Here, turn right and follow the path alongside the river downstream towards Eastgate village, passing the lovely Turry Wheel waterfall. The path eventually enters a caravan park near the village. Walk through this and exit onto the road, going left downhill to the A688 (2).

Note: the above section of riverside path can be very wet and could be difficult to follow when the burn is in spate. An alternative route would be to walk along the road to reach Eastgate village.

Go left past the pub and cross the footbridge, then turn immediately left and walk up the lane towards the village hall. Keep straight on along the lane past the hall, then pass in front of Holme House, staying on the track to Hole House Farm. Take the track on the right leading up into the woods at the farm, continuing along the track through fields/ woods until you reach a footbridge across Brandon Walls Cleugh (3).

Cross the footbridge and continue walking upstream alongside Rookhope Burn, passing the buildings/remains of some old quarry workings in the woods until you reach another footbridge, this time over Rookhope Burn itself. Go left over this to join the road, then turn right and follow the road back to Rookhope village.

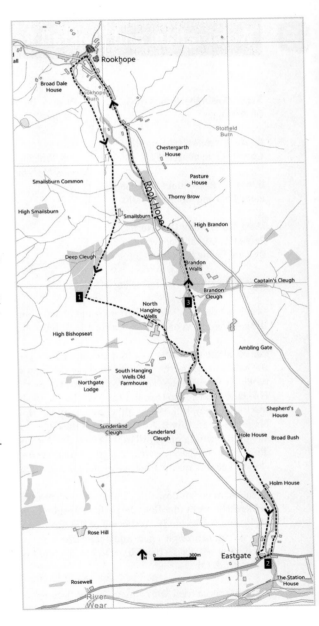

Wolsingham and Tunstall Reservoir

START Wolsingham, DL13 3DG, GR NZ075375

DISTANCE 7 miles/11.3km with 1,075ft/325m of ascent

SUMMARY A strenuous walk mainly along field and moorland paths

MAPS OS Explorer OL31 North Pennines; OS Landranger 92 Barnard Castle & Richmond

PARKING Demesne Mill picnic area car park

WHERE TO EAT AND DRINK The Black Bull, Wolsingham, To1388-527332, www.blackbullwolsingham.co.uk

A walk around the Tunstall valley, offering fine views throughout.

Leave the car park via the entrance and go left along the B6296 as far as the road junction on the left, leading to Holywood (1).

Go left along this as far as a footpath marker on the right. Go through the gate and follow the path uphill along the right edge of the field. After passing through trees, aim diagonally left across the field towards Baal Hill House farm. Go through the gates beside the barn and follow the track leading uphill. Where this forks, keep left through trees along a broad track. Stay on this as it traverses the edge of the moors, ignoring any paths leading off uphill to the right. Enter a wooded area and go left down a slippery stony path, then go right across a stream and exit the woods, keeping on the track as far the farm at Backstone Bank (2).

At the farm go left downhill, and at a set of stone pillars leave the road and go right to follow the path alongside the reservoir through Backstone Bank woods. At the end of the woods cross a stile onto a road, then go right through a gate and keep right to follow a track through a clearing uphill. Pass a black barn to reach a junction of paths at the top of the climb (3).

Go right onto a track into Ninety Acre Allotment, and stay on this as it heads south through rough pastures to start with and then open moorlands. After passing old quarry workings, the track starts to descend and becomes walled at Thistlewood La. Keep on downhill to a gate, where you come to a tarmac road. Keep straight ahead downhill, passing a number of houses/farms, then at the junction with the B6296 turn right and walk along the footpath to point (1).

Retrace the outward route back to the car park.

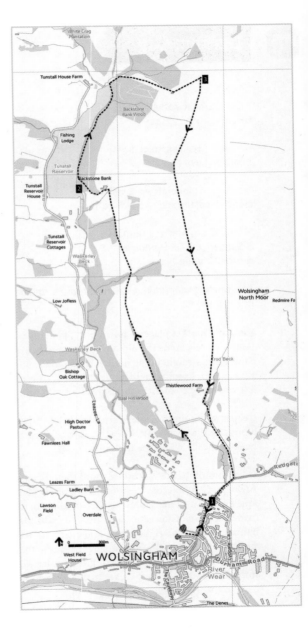

Start Durham Market Place, DH1 3PN, GR NZ274425

Distance 6¾ miles/10.9km with 88oft/265m of ascent

Summary A moderate walk mainly along woodland and riverside paths

Maps OS Explorer 308 Durham & Sunderland; OS Landranger 88 Newcastle upon Tyne

Parking Various pay and display car parks in Durham

Where to eat and drink Various outlets around the market place

A fascinating walk, linking various hospitals founded in Durham by the early Prince Bishops.

From the market place go north past St Nicholas's church onto Claypath. Follow this as far as the old post office, and turn left onto Providence Row. Keep straight along here to reach The Sands on the banks of the River Wear, keeping right along the road. At the end of the houses keep left where the road forks to reach a footpath sign (**1**).

Keep straight on to Kepier Farm. Here, take the path on the left alongside the riverbank to reach a gate on a track, turn right and walk back to the farm and the footpath sign (**1**).

Go left uphill beside the houses, and then through woods to reach the A690; go right to cross the footbridge over it. Keep left across the grassy area beyond and then take the narrow alley on the right down between houses to reach Gilesgate. Go across the road, then right to reach St Giles church. Pass to the right of this and over a stile, leading to a path down through woods. At the bottom go right along the road behind one of the colleges, and at the end of this building go left along a path leading down to the banks of the River Wear. Turn right and walk along the riverside path to the footbridge over the river (**2**).

Cross the footbridge, go left along the riverside path, passing the cricket ground to reach a car park just past the caravan site. Go left here through woods, keeping left at the next path junction to reach the river again. Stay alongside the river, heading for a footbridge. Don't cross this; instead, follow the path as it curves around to the right at Maiden Castle, to the A177. Cross this and follow the path through the woods. When a wooden paling fence appears on the left, keep an eye open for a stile leading into a field, and cross this and the field towards Houghall Farm. At the road go right over some steps onto an old tramway, which climbs up to join Hollingside La (**3**).

Go right along the lane and follow it to Greys College, passing the Botanical Gardens.

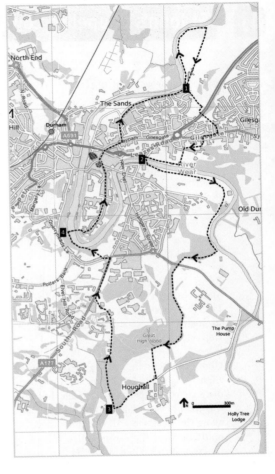

Pass between the accommodation blocks of the college to reach the main road, going right along this to a set of traffic lights. Go left and immediately cross the road, take the footpath into the park, keeping left in the park to enter the woods, then continue on to the banks of the River Wear. Go left along the riverside path to Prebends Bridge (**4**).

Cross the bridge and keep right uphill onto the North Bailey, then follow this back to the market place, passing the cathedral along the way.

St John's Chapel to Cowshill

START St John's Chapel, DL13 1QF, GR NY886378

DISTANCE 7¼ miles/11.7km with 1,060ft/320m of ascent

SUMMARY A strenuous walk along moorland/riverside paths and roads

MAPS OS Explorer OL31 North Pennines; OS Landranger 92 Barnard Castle & Richmond

PARKING Roadside parking

WHERE TO EAT AND DRINK The Chatterbox Café, St John's Chapel, T01388-537536

A walk over the high moorland on the north side of Weardale, returning along the banks of the River Wear.

From the parking area go left along the road into the village, then right along the road beside the green, which leads down to the village school. Just after passing this, go left over the stream, then right through a farmyard and across the field to Ponderlane Bridge. Cross this to some steps (**1**).

Climb the steps, and then go across another field to a minor road. Go slightly right to a farm track on the left, and follow this for a short distance till the path leads off left through a fallen down stone wall. It then climbs over fields to reach a stile, onto another minor road. Go left along the road to a walled track leading off on the right, and follow this uphill between high stone walls. Where the track levels out, it enters rough pastures. Keep following the right-hand edge fence/wall across these to reach another minor road. Go right along this to where it makes a sharp right turn beside the corner of a wood (**2**).

Leave the road and take the track on the left. Initially this goes alongside the wood, then after a gate it becomes a wall lane. Keep on the track, which becomes increasingly wet and muddy. Where the path starts to descend, keep right and follow it down through spoil heaps and old mine workings. On the valley floor, go left along the broad track to Cowshill village (**3**).

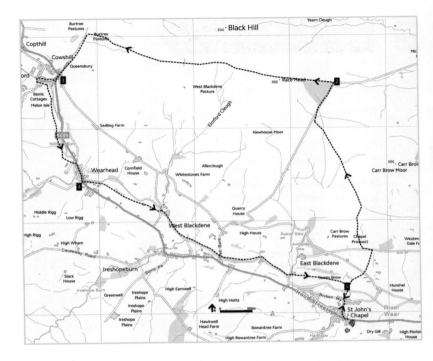

Go left along the A688, and then right between houses, keeping left to follow the road to Burtreeford. At the T-junction, go left over Burtreeford Bridge and then left through a gate onto a track, which follows the River Wear to the school at Wearhead. At the school go through the gate and then left to the A688, then turn right and walk through the village as far as Wearhead Bridge (4).

Just after crossing the bridge, go left along the riverside path, and follow this over several fields to a road. Go left, over a bridge to West Blackdene, and pass in front of the houses, continuing along the river to Coronation Bridge at Ireshopeburn. Cross the minor road and keep on the riverside path to near East Blackdene. Here, turn left over a footbridge into a farmyard, go through this and then through a gate beside the barn. Continue across meadows to reach (1).

Go right over Ponderlane Bridge and retrace your outward route back to the start.

Burnhope Reservoir

START Burnhope Reservoir, DL13 1DJ, GR NY886378

DISTANCE 7½ miles/12km with 1,250ft/380m of ascent

SUMMARY A strenuous walk over boggy moorlands, with no paths over the high sections

MAPS OS Explorer OL31 North Pennines; OS Landranger 92 Barnard Castle & Richmond

PARKING Roadside parking

WHERE TO EAT AND DRINK None

A challenging walk over the high moorlands between Teesdale and Weardale.

From the parking area go through the double metal gates in the wall and follow the path along the north shore of the reservoir. At first there are good views over the reservoir/Weardale from the path but these are blocked further along by a mature stand of conifers. Eventually you come to a footbridge over Burnhope Burn; cross this and leave the path, going right along the burn to a gate in a wall. Go through this and follow the burn upstream, pass a concrete bridge and keep on to another bridge a little further upstream. Join a track here and go left along it, and keep on till it forks (1).

Keep left at the fork and follow that track over the moors. At first it appears to be heading back towards the reservoir, but keep on it and it eventually turns to head along West Lang Tae. The track stops beside some grouse butts near the stream; continue uphill using the stream to guide you over the heather moorland. The going is rough at times and can be wet/boggy in places but keep on to reach the fence at the top (2).

Go left and follow the fence over the rough moorland, heading roughly south-east towards Great Stony Hill. On a clear day there are fine views over the North Pennines in all directions, especially from the trig point on Great Stony Hill, which is also the highest point on the walk

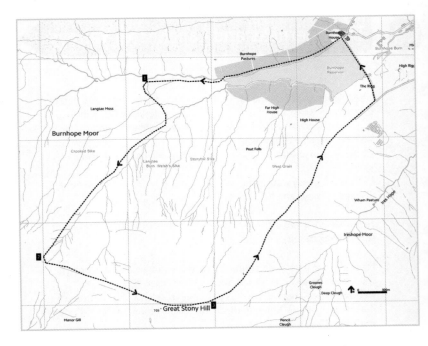

at 2,300 feet. Keep along the fence from here to reach another track at Coldberry End (**3**).

Go left along this track and follow it downhill back towards the reservoir. It eventually becomes surfaced. Keep on to where a road goes off on the left, go through the gate and follow the road down to a white gate, which leads back over the dam to the parking area.

Points of interest

The reservoir was created by the construction of an earth embankment dam across the valley of Burnhope Burn, a tributary of the River Wear, 1km above the village of Wearhead. Construction of the dam began in 1931 and was completed in 1937. Filling of the reservoir commenced in 1936 and resulted in the drowning of the former village of Burnhope.

The Deerness and Lanchester Valleys

START Broompark picnic area,
DH7 7RJ, GR NZ250415

DISTANCE 7½ miles/12km with
520ft/155m of ascent

SUMMARY An easy walk along
disused railways and field paths

MAPS OS Explorer 308 Durham
& Sunderland; OS Landranger 88
Newcastle upon Tyne

PARKING Picnic area car park

WHERE TO EAT AND DRINK None

This walk along two disused railway lines offers extensive views of the
surrounding countryside.

From the car park walk south through the picnic area to reach the
track bed of the old Deerness Railway, and turn right onto it. It's easy
walking. The River Deerness is down to your left in the bottom of
the wooded valley. Keep on until you reach the site of the old railway
station at Ushaw Moor (**1**).

Cross the road, go through the car park and cross the river to regain
the old track bed. Continue along, re-crossing the river on another
bridge. Shortly after this a bridge crosses over the track bed; go under it
and then take the path on the left going up to the bridge and road. Turn
left along the road and then directly across at the crossroads uphill
along Broadgate Rd, heading towards the grand buildings of Ushaw
Farm (**2**).

At the road junction turn right and walk along a short distance to
a track leaving off alongside a wall. Go left here along the track,
keeping ahead where it crosses a road to the corner of a hedge. Turn
right and follow the track along the field edge. At the next corner
go slightly right to a track going diagonally left through trees, and
at the bottom cross a stile. Go through a gate and follow the track
along the left side of the fields to a stile at the top of a bank. Cross
the stile and go diagonally right across the field, aiming for a line of
trees. Go left in front of them and go downhill to a gate to the left of
the trees (**3**).

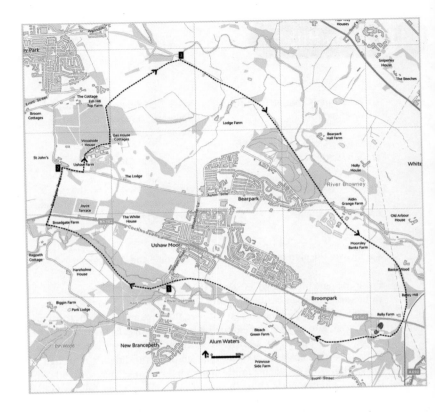

Go through the gate and turn right onto the Lanchester Railway path, which leads all the way back to the picnic area. Again, it's easy walking with grand views over the Durham countryside. Just after crossing the Bearpark road, keep left along a fenced path in front of the Aldin Grange farm shop. Keep right just after passing a pond to reach the East Coast mainline, go under the road bridge and keep on the old track bed to reach the picnic area, going right for the car park.

Noon Hill

START St John's Chapel, DL13 1QF, GR NY886378

DISTANCE 7¾ miles/12.5km with 1,400ft/425m of ascent

SUMMARY A strenuous walk along riverside paths and roads, and pathless moorland

MAPS OS Explorer OL31 North Pennines; OS Landranger 92 Barnard Castle & Richmond

PARKING Roadside parking

WHERE TO EAT AND DRINK The Chatterbox Café, St John's Chapel, T01388-537536

A walk over the high moorlands between Teesdale and Weardale.

From the parking area go left along the road into the village, going right along the road beside the green, which leads down to the village school. Just after passing this go left over the stream, then right through a farmyard and across the field to Ponderlane Bridge. Cross this to some steps, but don't go up them; instead, turn left and follow the path across fields towards a large barn. Pass to the left of this and then go through the yard in front to reach a footbridge over a stream. Cross this and then go right upstream along the banks of the River Wear, following the Weardale Way. Keep on until you reach a minor road, turn left on this to cross Coronation Bridge, then go right at the junction with the A689 and walk along this through Ireshopeburn village to where the main road takes a sharp right turn (1).

Leave the A689 and go left uphill on the road between the houses. At the T-junction keep straight ahead and continue along the road to Ireshope Plains. Here, the road ends. Keep on through the farmyard onto a track, and follow this over rough pastures to reach a gate in a wall, giving access to the open moorland (2).

Go through this and then continue uphill over pathless moorlands, roughly due south, to reach the corner of a fence on Noon Hill. Go left along the fence and follow it over the peaty/boggy ground to the summit of the St John's Chapel/Langdon Beck road at Harthope Head. Cross the

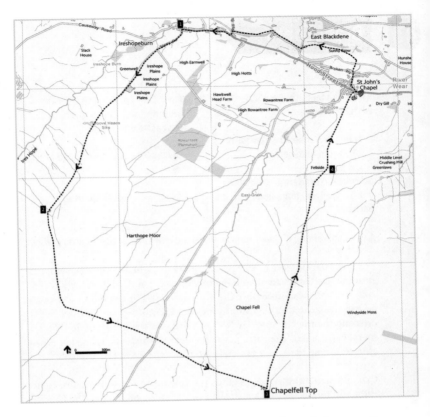

road and keep on following the fence line to eventually reach the summit of Chapelfell Top (3). The views over Teesdale, Weardale and the North Pennines are outstanding on a clear day.

Leave the summit, heading roughly north over more peaty/boggy ground. Where the descent back down into Weardale begins, aim towards the currick, and then keep on in the same direction, still going downhill, to reach the corner of a wall. Go left down the wall to a track, then go right along this to a gate in the wall (4).

Go through this and follow the walled track downhill back to St John's Chapel, to emerge beside the cattle market. From there it's a short walk back along the A689 to the car park.

Brancepeth

Start Brancepeth, DH7 8DL, GR NZ219382

Distance 8½ miles/13.7km with 460ft/140m of ascent

Summary A moderate walk along disused railway lines and riverside paths

Maps OS Explorer 308 Durham & Sunderland; OS Landranger 88 Newcastle upon Tyne

Parking Car park beside old railway line

Where to eat and drink None

A walk combining disused railway lines and a section of the Weardale Way.

From the parking area, go right along the track bed of the disused Brandon to Bishop Auckland railway line, which used to mainly carry coal and coke wagons before the line was closed in 1964. It now provides an easy walking/cycling route along the valley. Keep on the track bed, crossing the road at Stockley Bridge, until you reach a set of double metal gates across the path. Leave the old railway here and go left down alongside a hedge across two fields to reach the A690 (**1**).

Cross the road and go left as far as the entrance to the farm shop. Turn right and follow the track past the shop, keeping on to pass The Grange. At the end of the track, go through a gate into the field, walk downhill along the right edge of the field, go through the gate at the bottom and continue in the same direction to reach the banks of the River Wear. Cross the stile and go left on the riverside path. Stay on this to reach Page Bank Bridge (**2**).

Cross Whitworth La and continue following the River Wear downstream. It's easy walking along the riverbanks, with fine views. Keep on until you pass under a double set of overhead power lines; shortly after this the path leaves the riverside and cuts left across a rough pasture (**3**).

Go left along the lane, which curves around the back of houses at Holywell Hall. Join a surfaced lane, which leads uphill in about a mile

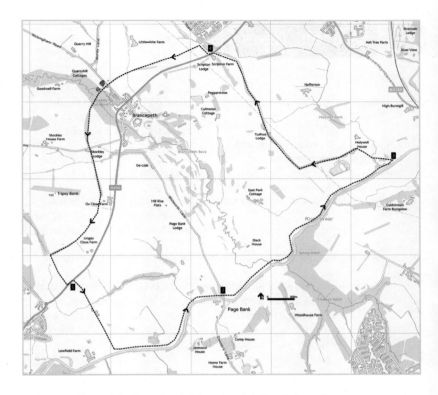

to Scripton Farm (**4**). Cross the A690 again, go left and then almost immediately right into the woods, following a path through the trees to emerge onto a disused railway line. Go left along this and follow it back to the car park.

Points of interest

A succession of buildings has been on the site of Brancepeth Castle. The first was a Norman castle built by the Bulmers, which was rebuilt by the Nevilles in the late fourteenth century. It was owned by the Neville family for many years, until it was confiscated in 1569 by the Crown following the family's involvement in the Rising of the North.

Elephant Trees

START **Wolsingham, DL13 3AF,
GR NZ047372**

DISTANCE **9½ miles/15.3km with
1,040ft/315m of ascent**

SUMMARY **A strenuous walk along
riverside/moorland paths and roads**

MAPS **OS Explorer OL31 North
Pennines; OS Landranger 92
Barnard Castle & Richmond**

PARKING **Roadside parking in the
market place**

WHERE TO EAT AND DRINK **The Black
Bull, Wolsingham, T01388-527332,
www.blackbullwolsingham.co.uk**

A mixed walk, including a wander along the edge of the high moorlands.

From the market place go right along the A688 and take the road on the
left, signposted to Hamsterley Forest and the Weardale Railway. Cross
Wolsingham Bridge (1). Just before the railway line, go right over a stile
onto a path running between the railway tracks and the River Wear. Stay
on this until you reach a caravan park (2).

Keep right through the caravan park on the riverside path to eventually
rejoin the railway line, which again you should follow to a footbridge
across the River Wear. Don't cross this; instead, keep left and follow the
track through the remains of the old Broadwood Quarry, which is now a
nature reserve, to reach a minor road (3).

Turn left and walk along the road uphill, past the school. Where the
road forks, keep left towards White Kirkley. Continue climbing along
the road, the views improving all the time as height is gained, to reach
Allotment House. Pass this and continue to the top of the climb and the
moorlands via a gate in the wall (4).

Go left along the wall. The Elephant Trees are clearly visible ahead now,
though from this perspective they look nothing special, just like any
other clump of trees. It's easy walking along the edge of the heather
moors – to your left are great views down into Weardale and on the
right rolling heather moors lead to Hamsterley and, in the far distance,

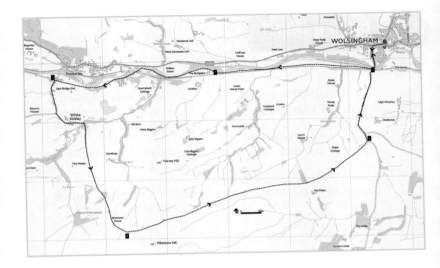

the Cleveland Hills. Eventually the moors are left behind and the track continues across rough pastures to reach the Wolsingham/Hamsterley road at the top of Wear Bank (**5**).

Go left downhill, keeping left again at the next junction, and walk down the road back to Wolsingham Bridge (**1**). Cross the bridge and retrace your outward route back to the market place.

Points of interest

The Elephant Trees are so named because when seen from a distance they look like a herd of elephants crossing the skyline in single file, linked tail to trunk. Sadly the number of trees is slowly declining over time.

Page Bank

START The Batts, Bishop Auckland, DL14 7QE, GR NZ210303

DISTANCE 10 miles/16km with 750ft/225m of ascent

SUMMARY A easy but long walk along riverside paths and old railway lines

MAPS OS Explorer 305 Bishop Auckland; OS Landranger 93 Middlesbrough

PARKING Parking area beside the River Wear

WHERE TO EAT AND DRINK Various places in Bishop Auckland

A walk combining riverside paths and disused railway lines.

From the parking area, go along the riverside path towards the Newton Cap Viaduct, going under this to the 'old' bridge. Go right over this and then immediately right again along a track back under the viaduct. Stay on this track as far as a junction, then go left uphill to reach a car park on the old Brandon to Bishop Auckland railway line. Go right along the old track bed and continue for about 2½ miles to where a road crosses the track (1).

Leave the railway and go right along the road, past a cottage. Where it makes a sharp right turn, leave it by going left through a gate and down across a field. At the bottom go left over a stile and follow the path alongside a stream to the banks of the River Wear. Go left, downstream, and follow the path along the river to the picnic area at Jubilee Bridge. Go under the bridge and continue along the riverbank to eventually reach Page Bank Bridge (2).

Go right over the bridge along the Whitworth Rd, continue as far as the entrance to the church, and here cross the road, going right along a track. Stay on the track, passing Hagg Farm, where the track takes a sharp right turn beside the stream. Leave it and go left over fields to join another disused railway line near some houses. Go right along the track bed, cross a road, then pass the platform of the old Byers Green Station. Pass under a large steel bridge before climbing up to the road at Binchester. Cross the road and keep on the track bed, passing the village to reach a pair of stone bridges over the track (3).

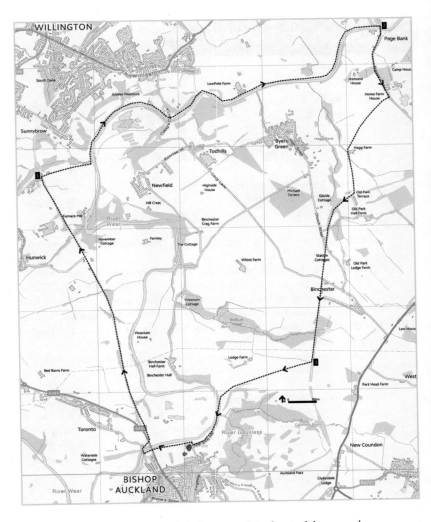

Go under the first, and then go left along a path in front of the second, which doubles back to take you up to the top of the first bridge. Go left over the bridge and then across fields, heading downhill towards the Auckland Deer Park. Don't enter the park; stay on the outside of the park, following the field edge to reach a road. Go left along this back to the car park at The Batts.

Stanhope Common

START Parkhead Station, DL13 2ES,
GR NY999432

DISTANCE 10 miles/16km with
1,300ft/395m of ascent

SUMMARY A strenuous walk mainly
along disused railway lines/
moorland tracks

MAPS OS Explorer 307 Consett &
Derwent Reservoir; OS Landranger
87 Hexham & Haltwhistle

PARKING Picnic area car park

WHERE TO EAT AND DRINK Parkhead
Station tea rooms, T01388-526464,
www.parkheadstation.co.uk

An airy walk over the moors surrounding the headwaters of Stanhope Burn.

From the car park walk back to the B6278 and go right uphill for a short
distance to a footpath marker on the left. Leave the road here and climb
the embankment on the left to join the bed of a disused railway line. You
can now see nearly all the walk laid out ahead of you around the head
of the valley. The first section of track bed is eroded in places and there
are a few wet sections, but once the access track to a farm is crossed
it becomes a hard gravel surface and much easier to walk along. Keep
straight ahead until a track comes in from the right (**1**).

Keep on the track bed, aiming for Longlaw End and ignoring the track
going off on the left. At Longlaw End you reach the top of the Boltlaw
Incline and the remains of the engine sheds, which housed the engines
to pull the trucks up from Rookhope in the valley below. Pass the old
buildings and start downhill towards the valley bottom, but only as far
as the track junction on the left, just after passing a sheepfold (**2**).

Go left here and follow the track as it curves and climbs gently
uphill around Longlaw End, then drops down to the shooting lodge
beside Smiddy Burn, which sits in a small wooded area with lots of
rhododendron bushes around it. The track continues over the moors to
reach Park Plantation. Keep on until you come to a T-junction in front of
a wall (**3**).

Go right through a gate onto a walled track and then left at the first

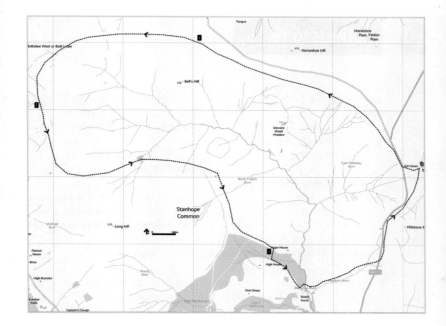

junction near High House, following this track alongside the woods to a three-way junction. Here, go left downhill to cross Stanhope Burn, entering an area of disused mine buildings. Just before the first building on the left, go left uphill on a track through gorse bushes, and then alongside a wall to reach a metal gate. Go through the gate and keep right on the track as it climbs up through Heathery Burn to meet the B6278. Cross this and go left uphill along the line of the old Weatherhill Incline, and at the top pass through an area of spoil heaps to join the Waskerley Way, which leads back to the car park.

Points of interest

Parkhead Station: the railway was opened in 1834 to transport limestone from the quarries above Stanhope in Weardale and coal from the various collieries in North Durham to South Shields right through until railway traffic ceased on this original Stanhope and Tyne route from 1 May 1969.

Cotherstone

Start The Hagg, Cotherstone, DL12 9QE, GR NZ011200

Distance 2 miles/3.2km with 165ft/50m of ascent

Summary An easy walk along field and riverside paths

Maps OS Explorer OL31 North Pennines; OS Landranger 92 Barnard Castle & Richmond

Parking Parking area next to recreation area

Where to eat and drink The Red Lion, Cotherstone, T01833-650236, www.theredlionhotel.blogspot.com

A lovely short walk around the environs of Cotherstone village.

From the parking area go right uphill back towards the village, keeping right where this forks to reach the B6277. Go left along here and walk through the village to the primary school. **(1)**

Here, go left across the bottom of the village green, pass between the houses and go over the stile ahead into the field. Keep along the left-hand edge of the field, passing the Friends Meeting house, and continue in the same direction over more fields. Shortly after crossing a footbridge you will join Demesne La; go straight ahead across the field. Go right along the edge of the woods to a stile in the field corner. Cross this and go downhill alongside the hedge to Cooper House. **(2)**

Go left along a slanting path down across the field to cross a footbridge over a stream, then across the field beyond to enter woods via a gate. Go steeply up steps through the woods to a gate beside some wooden sheds. **(3)**

Go through the gate and then go through another gate immediately on the right onto a lane alongside the edge of a field; keep on this where it crosses a surfaced lane to enter more woods. At the end of the woods, go steeply down some wooden steps towards a footbridge. Don't cross this; instead, go left following the lane alongside a stone wall back to the parking area.

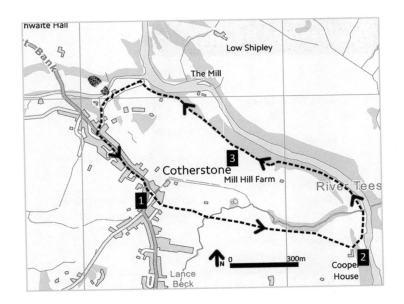

nwaite Hall

t-Bank

Low Shipley

The Mill

3

Cotherstone

Mill Hill Farm

River Tees

1

N   0   300m

Lance
Beck

2

Coope
House

Points of interest

Cotherstone has been an agricultural community since Anglo-Saxon times. A local speciality is Cotherstone cheese, similar in style to Wensleydale.

Bowlees and Holwick

Start Bowlees Visitor Centre, DL12 0XF, GR NY907282

Distance 2½ miles/4km with 260ft/80m of ascent

Summary An easy walk along field and riverside paths

Maps OS Explorer OL31 North Pennines; OS Landranger 92 Barnard Castle & Richmond

Parking Park and donate parking

Where to eat and drink Bowlees Visitor Centre, T01833-622145, www.visitbowlees.org.uk

A walk around the villages of Bowlees, Newbiggin and Holwick.

Leave the car park along the track going uphill behind the brick building, cross a cattle grid, and stay on the track to the next gate. Leave the track here and go right across the fields to Hood Gill. Cross a stile and then continue across two more fields to reach a road, then go right along this downhill into Newbiggin village. Take the first road on the right and walk along this to the B6277 **(1)**.

Cross the road and go right and take the path heading left across the field, to a stile in the far corner. Cross the stile to enter a narrow walled track, and follow it downhill to a footbridge over Bowlee Beck. Cross the bridge and go diagonally left across the field, through a gap in the wall, and continue ahead to Scoberry Bridge. Cross the River Tees via the footbridge to join the Pennine Way, albeit briefly, as you leave it almost immediately by crossing a stile over a fence on the left. Aim for the gap in the wall at the right end of the field, and then go left uphill across two more fields to reach the road. Go right along this through Holwick village **(2)**.

Keep right where the road turns sharp right at the end of the village, and follow the road downhill to a cattle grid. Cross this and then go diagonally right across the field heading towards Low Force and the Wynch Bridge. Cross three more fields to reach a kissing gate near the suspension bridge over the River Tees. Low Force waterfall is just upstream from the bridge, although good views can be found from the

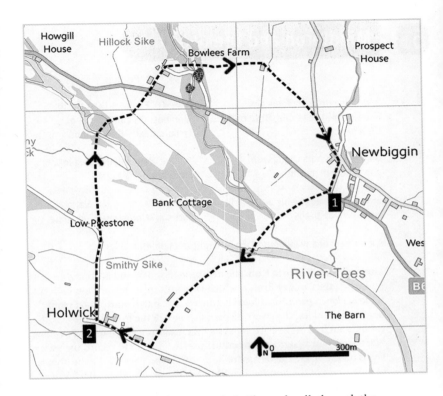

viewing area next to the bridge. Cross the bridge and walk through the trees, climbing to a gate/stile, cross this and then over the two fields beyond to reach the B6277 and Bowlees village. Cross the road and take the first lane on the left; ahead can be seen the old chapel, which is now the visitor centre. Go through the yard of the centre, up the steps, following the path to more steps, which take you down to a footbridge and the car park.

Points of interest

Bowlees Visitor Centre, T01833-622145
www.visitbowlees.org.uk

Middleton and Leekworth

START The drinking fountain, Middleton-in-Teesdale, DL12 0SH, GR NY947254

MAPS OS Explorer OL31 North Pennines; OS Landranger 92 Barnard Castle & Richmond

DISTANCE 2½ miles/4km with 260ft/80m of ascent

PARKING Roadside parking in Middleton-in-Teesdale

SUMMARY An easy walk along field and riverside paths

WHERE TO EAT AND DRINK Various places in Middleton-in-Teesdale

A little gem of a walk around the environs of Middleton village.

Turn left into Bridge St from the drinking fountain and go along it towards the County Bridge, which was built in 1811; the views of Kirkcarrion, a prominent local landmark, are particularly good from here. Go left along the riverside path just before the bridge – the cobbled surface of the path suggests that it was once well used. Pass the Northumbrian Water river monitoring station, used to record the water levels on the river. The terrace of houses that you pass used to be homes of employees of the London Lead Mining Company. The path continues along the riverside, going past a low stone wall in the riverbank. Not far after this, you come to a caravan site; continue past it. The path climbs through gorse bushes where the river starts to make a long slow bend (**1**).

Leave the riverside path here and go left across a field to a stream, then left again, heading along a flat section to pass a black barn. Continue across a field towards the corner of a wall, cross a small flagstone bridge and, keeping the wall on your right, go along to a stile beside a gate. Cross and then go along the road through the houses to the B6282. Go left along this and walk along the village green back to the drinking fountain.

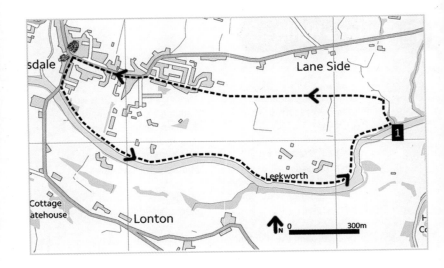

Points of interest

Middleton-in-Teesdale is the main centre for Upper Teesdale, and developed largely as a result of the lead mining industry. It was here that the London Lead Mining Company established its North of England headquarters in 1815.

Kings Walk

START The drinking fountain, Middleton-in-Teesdale, DL12 0SH, GR NY947254

DISTANCE 3 miles/4.8km with 540ft/165m of ascent

SUMMARY A moderate walk along field and riverside paths

MAPS OS Explorer OL31 North Pennines; OS Landranger 92 Barnard Castle & Richmond

PARKING Roadside parking in Middleton-in-Teesdale

WHERE TO EAT AND DRINK Various places in Middleton-in-Teesdale

A short walk around the Hudeshope valley to the north of Middleton village.

From the drinking fountain go along the Market Place to the Teesdale Hotel, where the road forks (**1**). Keep left along the B6277 to cross the bridge over Hudeshope Beck. Where the B6277 curves sharp left, go right uphill. When almost at the top of the hill go right up stone steps along a path between houses; at the end of the houses you join a track. Go through a metal gate and keep left alongside the wall where the track splits, continuing through the woods to reach a kissing gate in the wall. Go through this into a field, continuing across the fields aiming for the houses of Aukside in the distance. As you approach the houses, go through the gate to the left of the large farmhouse which gives access to a lane (**2**).

Go right along this, passing through the farm buildings. Where the lane turns sharp left cross a stile on the right beside a barn, stay alongside the wall to the field corner, then go diagonally right across the next field. At first the descent is gradual but steepens as you near How Gill. Ford the stream at the bottom and go through a gate in the wall onto a track. Go right on this to a bridge over Hudeshope Beck (**3**).

Cross the bridge, noting the large lime kilns slightly to the left after crossing the bridge. You are now on Beck Rd. Follow this back along the Hudeshope valley through the trees to eventually reach the Snaisgill road opposite a terrace of houses. Go right downhill along the road back to the Teesdale Hotel (**1**).

Go left back along the Market Place to the drinking fountain.

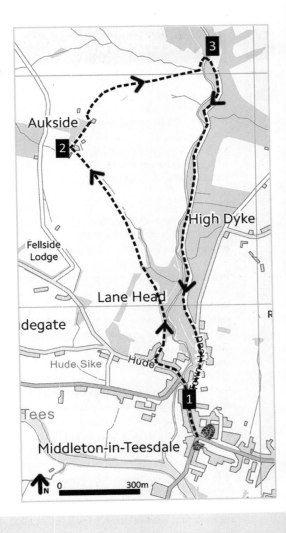

Points of interest

Limestone from the nearby Skeers Quarry was burnt in the kilns near Beck Rd and the lime was used to improve the soil in the fields around the village.

Hamsterley Forest

START Forest Visitor Centre,
DL13 3NL, GR NZ092311

DISTANCE Short walk – 3 miles/4.8km
with 400ft/120m of ascent; long
walk – 5 miles/8km with 800ft/240m
of ascent

SUMMARY Easy walks mainly along
forest tracks, which can be muddy
in places

MAPS OS Explorer OL31 North
Pennines; OS Landranger 92
Barnard Castle & Richmond

PARKING Pay and display car parking

WHERE TO EAT AND DRINK Hamsterley
Forest Tearooms, T01388-488822
(open Mon–Sun 10–5)

Two short walks along waymarked trails through Hamsterley Forest.

From the signpost in the car park which indicates the start of the trails,
go right along Bedburn Beck until you reach the footbridge, go left over
the bridge and follow the path through the stands of mature conifers
until the next bridge across the river. Don't cross this; instead, turn left
and follow the forest track uphill to the T-junction (1).

For the short walk go right along the track – the trail is marked by black
arrows on a square, yellow background. Continue along this until you
reach a tarmac road. Go right downhill along the road until you see a
track on the right; take this, and at the bottom join a cross-track and go
left. This splits almost immediately; keep right and go downhill to reach
a wooden bridge. Don't cross this; keep right initially along the banks
of Bedburn Beck, then climb through the trees until a marker indicates
the path going left down to stone steps, leading to another bridge across
the stream at the Redford car park. Cross the bridge and go through the
car park to the forest drive; turn right and follow this to the *Green Man*
sculpture (5).

Continue along the forest drive until it splits. Go left uphill, passing in
front of some houses, and just after these pass a green gate and turn right
onto a forest track. Follow this until the T-junction at the end. Turn right
and go along a path to reach some steps beside the visitor centre. Go

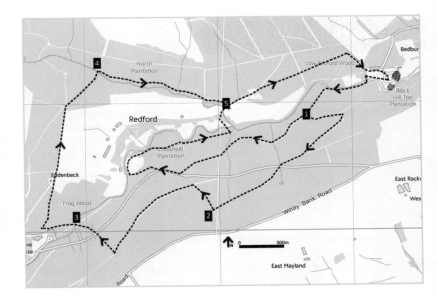

down these to re-join the forest drive, and go left past the tearooms to reach the car park.

For the longer walk, which is waymarked by black arrows on an orange background, go left at (1) until a marker indicates a path heading up through the trees. Go right and follow this until you reach a track; go right again and follow the track to a tarmac road (2). Go directly across the road and follow the track until you reach a footpath marker. Go right down through the trees; at the bottom, go left along a track to another footpath marker. Go right along a path, and at the bottom turn left to reach the forest drive/bridge (3). Cross the bridge and take a path on the right to reach a footbridge. Don't cross; go right uphill, passing a cottage, and continue along the track until you come across large stones across it. Go right downhill, and cross a footbridge to reach a ruined building (4). Take the path on your right and follow this along Ayhope Beck to reach Philip Townsend's *Green Man* sculpture (5).

Pecknell Woods

START Scar Top, Barnard Castle,
DL12 8PW, GR NZ049166

DISTANCE 3¼ miles/5.2km with
290ft/90m of ascent

SUMMARY An easy walk along the
Teesdale Way on field/riverside
paths

MAPS OS Explorer OL31 North
Pennines; OS Landranger 92
Barnard Castle & Richmond

PARKING Pay and display car parking

WHERE TO EAT AND DRINK Various
pubs/cafés available in Barnard
Castle

A most pleasant walk along the west bank of the River Tees.

From Scar Top – from where (on your left) the entrance to the eleventh-
century Barnard Castle can be seen – take the wide tarmac path on the
right, passing in front of the play area. Continue along it and keep left,
descending to the riverside in Flatts Wood and the footbridge across the
river. Go over this, with grand views of the river and castle, to reach the
Lartington Rd. Turn right and walk a short distance to a footpath sign
next to some cottages (1).

Go right here along a pleasant track running along the banks of the
river. After about ½ mile cross a cattle grid (2) and continue along the
track now through woods, passing a cottage on the right. Shortly after
this a marker post on the right takes you along a narrow grassy path
through pine trees to reach the track bed of the old Barnard Castle to
Kirby Stephen railway. Cross the track bed and a stile into a field, follow
the right-hand edge of this to a stile, cross this and go left along the
hedge to another stile. Cross this to join a road. Go right towards Towler
Hill Farm, staying on the track where it goes sharp left and continuing
across open fields for about ¼ mile until you reach a gate.

Turn left and go through a tunnel under the old railway into a field
beyond, following the right-hand edge to a track. Turn left along the
track towards a cottage, passed on the left. Cross the field behind the
cottage, aiming for a distant telegraph pole. Keep left to reach a gate into
the woods, and follow the grassy track which soon joins a road. Keep

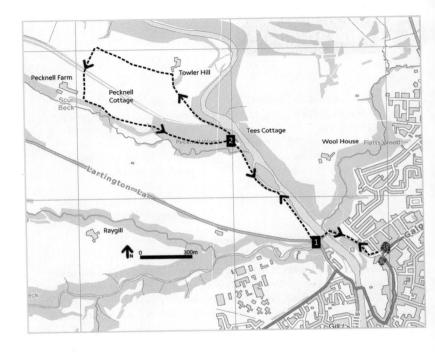

right and follow this back to the cattle grid (2). Go back along the track to the cottages and re-trace your outward route back over the footbridge and up to Scar Top.

Points of interest

It was from near Towler Hill Farm that the famous English painter J. M. W. Turner painted a view of Barnard Castle in 1816. This is one of many views he recorded on his travels through the area.

Kirkcarrion

START The drinking fountain,
Middleton-in-Teesdale, DL12 0SH,
GR NY947254

DISTANCE 3¼ miles/5.2km with
700ft/210m of ascent

SUMMARY An easy walk along field
and moorland paths

MAPS OS Explorer OL31 North
Pennines; OS Landranger 92
Barnard Castle & Richmond

PARKING Roadside parking in
Middleton-in-Teesdale

WHERE TO EAT AND DRINK Various
places in Middleton-in-Teesdale

A short walk around Teesdale's iconic landmark.

Turn left into Bridge St from the drinking fountain and go along it towards the County Bridge, which was built in 1811. The views of Kirkcarrion are particularly good from here. Cross the bridge, pass the cattle market and continue uphill along the B6277. At the junction go right along the Holwick road, and then immediately left through a gate. Go steeply uphill along a rough track and continue alongside the wall to reach a gate (1).

Go through the gate and where the track takes a sharp left bend leave it beside a cairn, taking a path across grass to reach a second gate. Go through this and leave the Pennine Way, which goes off to the right, staying straight ahead (no path) and heading for Rams Gill, the dry valley ahead. Continue up the gill to the stone wall at the head of it. Cross the stile and then across the pasture beyond to Greengates. Go left downhill, passing buildings to reach the Lunedale road (2).

Go left along the road to a footpath marker on the left. Leave the road and follow the track uphill, heading back up towards Kirkcarrion, to a gate. Go through the gate and go right along a grassy track, keeping left where this forks, to reach a gate. Go through this and continue downhill across rough pastures, with great views of Middleton village, to rejoin the outward route at (1). Re-trace the route back to Middleton.

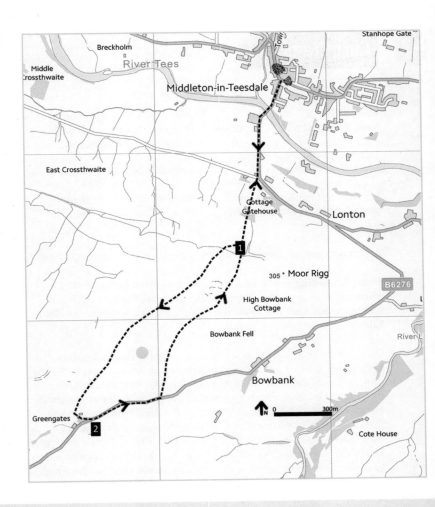

Points of interest

Kirkcarrion is a copse of pine trees, surrounded by a stone wall, on a hilltop near Middleton-in-Teesdale. The trees cover a tumulus which is said to be the burial place of a Bronze Age chieftain. The trees were planted by Elija Foster and his son Alan Foster of Lowside Farm in 1936.

Carr Crags

START Watson's Bridge, near
Newbiggin, DL12 0UF, GR NY910301

DISTANCE 3¼ miles/5.2km with
86oft/26om of ascent

SUMMARY A strenuous walk over wet
boggy moorlands with few paths

MAPS OS Explorer OL31 North
Pennines; OS Landranger 92
Barnard Castle & Richmond

PARKING Roadside parking

WHERE TO EAT AND DRINK None

A short walk over rough moorlands, visiting some ancient stone markings.

From the parking area, cross the road and go through the gate to the
right of the bridge. Follow the track alongside Flushiemere Beck to the
gate just below the ruins of the old mine building at Flushiemere House
(1).

Go through the gate and follow the track up to the ruined building,
keeping left where it forks along a grassy track as far as a stream coming
downhill from the right. Go right and follow this stream uphill. There is
no path and it can be very boggy/wet, and in places it almost disappears,
but it's clear enough to follow. Eventually the stream cuts across the
line of Carr Crags – it doesn't attain any great height; it's more of a
collection of boulders on the grassy moorland. The cup/ring markings
can be found amongst the rocks to the left of the path. The easiest way
to explore is to climb up to the top of the rocks and there is a faint path
running along the top edge. Continue up past the rocks, still following
the line of the stream initially. Where this disappears keep on in the
same direction up onto James's Hill, the highest point being a slightly
higher bit of ground over to the left. To the north are the vast boggy
wastes of Outberry Plain, and to the south grand views over Teesdale
and the high peaks of the Yorkshire Dales further south **(2)**.

Leave James's Hill by heading south-west across pathless moorlands. As
the ground starts to drop away a wall becomes visible in the distance –
you are aiming for the corner of this where it turns and runs downhill

to Flushiemere House. Eventually you will come to the top of another section of Carr Crags; carefully pick your way down through the boulders. This section is where you are likely to find unfinished millstones lying on the moors; a little exploring might be required but they are there. Keep on downhill over the grassy moorland to the wall corner (3).

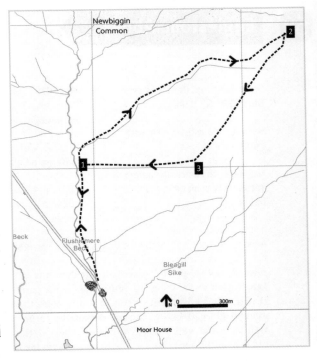

Go right downhill alongside the wall, which leads back to Flushiemere House. There are some wet sections that need to be negotiated, but keep on downhill. At the bottom, pass to the right of the sheep pens to join the track near the ruined building and back to the gate (1).

Retrace your outward route back to Watson's Bridge.

Points of interest

A number of cup and ring marks can be seen on a group of large rocks at Carr Crags. These marks probably have a geological origin and may not be man-made. The outcrop has been extensively quarried and a number of millstones can still be found laid around the bottom of the crags.

Egglestone Abbey

START Scar Top, Barnard Castle, DL12 8PW, GR NZ049166

DISTANCE 3½ miles/5.6km with 290ft/90m of ascent

SUMMARY An easy walk along the Teesdale Way on field/riverside paths

MAPS OS Explorer OL31 North Pennines; OS Landranger 92 Barnard Castle & Richmond

PARKING Various car parks available in Barnard Castle

WHERE TO EAT AND DRINK Various pubs/cafés available in Barnard Castle

A most pleasant walk along the banks of the River Tees.

From Scar Top, go left down alongside the walls of Barnard Castle, keeping left under the walls and following the path to the County Bridge. Don't cross this; stay on the north side of the river and walk left along Bridgegate to the Blue Bell pub on the corner of Thorngate. Turn right here and walk along Thorngate to the end, then pass between the old mill buildings and cross the River Tees via the footbridge. Go up the steps directly in front, keeping left where the path forks, onto The Lendings. Walk along this road to the end and then enter the caravan park (**1**).

Go right along the road through the park, to the entrance. Here, leave the road by going left over a stile to follow a path across three fields, joining a lane. Go left along the lane towards the abbey, keeping an eye open for Bow Bridge over Thorsgill Beck below the abbey – it's to the right of the new road bridge as you pass. To visit the abbey you would need to make a short detour along the road to the right. After visiting the abbey continue along the road to the traffic lights, at Abbey Bridge. Go left and cross the bridge (**2**).

Go left on the footpath leading down through the woods from the bridge to reach riverside meadows. Continue upstream alongside the river, with good views of the abbey, to pass beside the water treatment works (**3**).

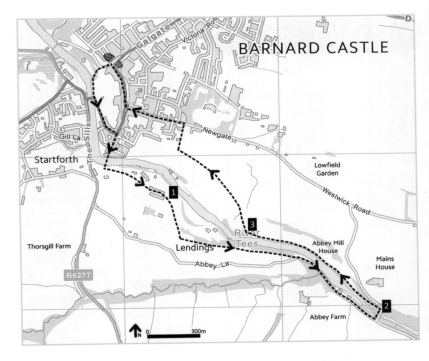

At the end of the works, go diagonally right across an open field to a kissing gate in the hedge. Go through this and then diagonally left towards the corner of the fence surrounding the playing fields, then aim right across the open area towards the wall, which will bring you to the end of Parsons Lonnen. Go right along this to Newgate, turn left and walk along to the Buttermarket. Turn right here onto the High St, and follow it back to Scar Top.

Points of interest

Ralph du Multon founded Egglestone Abbey of St Mary and St John the Baptist in 1196 for the Premonstratensian Order of Regular Canons. The remains of an old paper mill can be seen on the south bank of the river near to the abbey. Turner painted both the mill and abbey in the early nineteenth century when the mill was still working.

Butterknowle

START Quarry Lane, Butterknowle, DL13 5LL, GR NZ100255

DISTANCE 3½ miles/5.6km with 330ft/100m of ascent

SUMMARY A short, easy walk along field/riverside paths

MAPS OS Explorer OL31 North Pennines; OS Landranger 92 Barnard Castle & Richmond

PARKING Picnic area car park

WHERE TO EAT AND DRINK The Royal Oak, Butterknowle, T01388-718903

A pleasant walk along field paths to the River Gaunless.

From the car park go right along Quarry La to the junction with Copley La. Go left and then take the second track on the right, signposted to High West Garth farm. Where it splits, go right and then immediately left along a grassy track to pass some farm buildings. At the end, go through a gate and then straight across the field to reach the edge of the woods (1).

Go left over a stile and along the top of a bank to reach a stone wall, then turn right downhill on a track into an open area. Go through the gate in the wall on the left and ford the River Gaunless. Go right up through gorse bushes along a path to reach the corner of a wall. Go left along the wall to join the track bed of the old Bishop Auckland to Barnard Castle railway. Continue along this until you reach a bridge. Don't cross this; instead, go down steeply to the left to a footbridge and re-cross the river. A path leads diagonally left up through bushes to a gate, and then across a field to Lower West Garth Farm. Enter the yard via double metal gates and pass beside the farmhouse onto the access track, which continues to Copley La (2).

Cross the road and go right to a footpath sign. Here, go left over three fields to Grewburn Beck, cross this and follow the path through the remains of the old Diamond Colliery to join the road through the village. Turn left and walk through Butterknowle until the road takes a sharp right turn. Here, leave the road and cross the field towards the barn/houses, passing between these to reach Quarry La, and go left back to the car park.

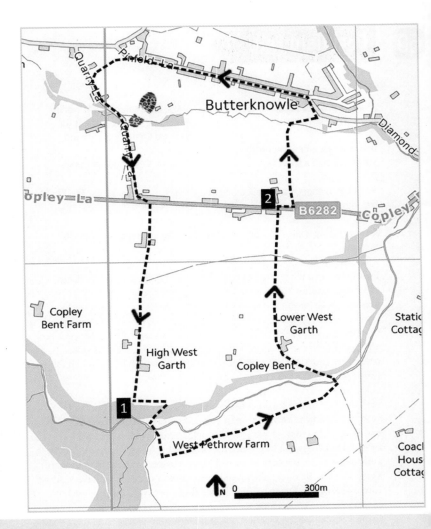

Points of interest

Diamond Bank: a stone slab stands at the west end of
Butterknowle village, marked with an arrow, and marks the spot
where local policeman Sergeant Smith was murdered in 1884.

Cockfield Fell

Start Hollymoor, Cockfield, DL13 5HF, GR NZ115242

Distance 3¾ miles/6km with 390ft/120m of ascent

Summary A short, easy walk along moorland/riverside paths

Maps OS Explorer OL31 North Pennines; OS Landranger 92 Barnard Castle & Richmond

Parking Roadside car park

Where to eat and drink The Kings Head, Cockfield, To1388-718176

An interesting walk over Cockfield Fell, passing mining and industrial remains.

From the car park go right along the road and then left at the first junction, passing Hollymoor Farm, to another road junction. Turn right here and walk along the road to a cattle grid (**1**).

Continue along the road through Cockfield village. At the far end, just after passing the church, go left along a track, which is signposted to the cemetery, and keep left when you join a road, which leads to Fell Houses (**2**).

Pass in front of the cottages and continue straight ahead, initially alongside a fence then over open ground. Where the ground steepens and drops towards the stream, keep left and descend to cross a footbridge across the River Gaunless. After crossing the river, go left and follow the track bed of the old Haggerleases branch line upstream as far as Skew Bridge, passing the remains of a once impressive viaduct across the valley. On reaching Skew Bridge, cross it and then go left over a stile, crossing an open area to an old metal fence. Go right here along a track passing beside the water treatment works to reach a road (**3**).

Go left uphill from the junction and then, at a footpath sign on the left, head back across the open fell towards Cockfield. Cross the track bed of the Bishop Auckland to Barnard Castle railway and then pass under power lines, keeping on in the same direction until you reach a fence

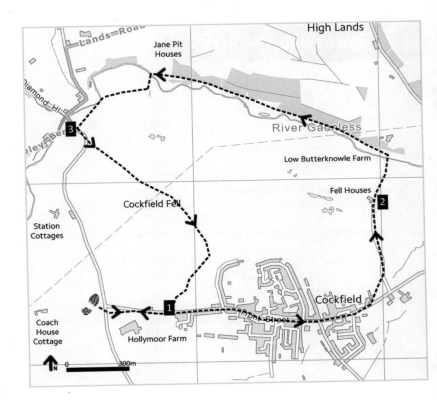

behind the village. Go right along the fence to reach a gate beside some sheds (**1**).

Go through the gate, turn right and retrace the outward route back to the car park.

Points of interest

Haggerleases branch line was specifically built to serve the Butterknowle and Marsfield Colliery. It closed in 1910, along with the whole complex of industrial activity in this small valley.

Bowes and The Rigg

START **Bowes, DL2 9HU,
GR NY995135**

DISTANCE **4 miles/6.4km with
360ft/110m of ascent**

SUMMARY **An easy walk over heather
moorlands and field paths**

MAPS **OS Explorer OL31 North
Pennines; OS Landranger 92
Barnard Castle & Richmond**

PARKING **Small parking area opposite
the village hall**

WHERE TO EAT AND DRINK **None**

An excellent walk with superb views of the River Greta Valley.

From the car park go left along the road towards Gilmonby village, cross
over the River Greta via Gilmonby Bridge, and just after this there is a
footpath marker on the left (**1**).

Cross the stile and walk straight ahead across three fields to reach
the corner of a wood. Go along the edge of this to enter Tom Gill
Plantation. A stream runs through it; cross this via a footbridge and
exit the woods. Go diagonally right across the field to a gate, pass
through this and keep on in the same direction up towards Howlugill,
crossing How Low Gill along the way. Pass to the left of buildings to
join a track. Go left along this and, where it turns 90 degrees right,
leave it and go across a stile into fields. Keep on in the same direction
across more fields to Plover Hall. Go through a wooded area just before
the buildings, and exit onto a road. Turn left along the road, and stay
on this heading towards White Close Hill Farm. Just before the farm
a footpath goes off right across a field to West Ling; take this, cross the
wall and stream, and enter the farmyard. Pass between the buildings to
a gate in the wall (**2**).

Exit the yard via the gate onto open moorland, and go right along a
track through the rough grass (this can be wet in places). Keep on this to
reach a gate in the wall, which leads onto a walled lane. Go through the
gate and follow the walled lane to Quarry Hill, where it joins a surfaced
road. Go left along the road and, after about a mile, go right at the road
junction to reach Gilmonby village and point (**1**).

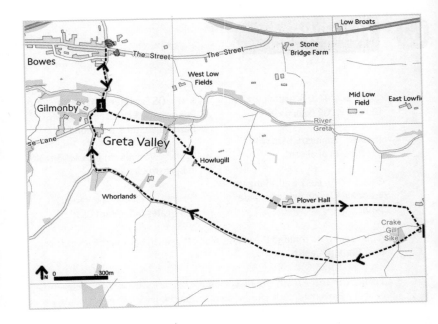

Retrace your outward route back to Bowes village. A short detour to Mill Force waterfall can be made, just after crossing Gilmonby Bridge: go left along a track through the woods and follow this to the waterfall.

Points of interest

The views from near White Close Hill Farm over the Greta valley include: Bowes village, the castle and, beyond, Mickle Fell, which at 2,591ft is the highest point in County Durham.

Flatts Wood

START Scar Top, Barnard Castle, DL12 8PW, GR NZ049166

DISTANCE 4 miles/6.4km with 370ft/110m of ascent

SUMMARY An easy walk along the Teesdale Way on field/riverside paths

MAPS OS Explorer OL31 North Pennines; OS Landranger 92 Barnard Castle & Richmond

PARKING Various car parks available in Barnard Castle

WHERE TO EAT AND DRINK Various pubs/cafés in Barnard Castle

A pleasant walk through the woods along the north bank of the River Tees, near Barnard Castle.

From Scar Top – from where (on your left) the entrance to the eleventh-century Barnard Castle can be seen – take the wide tarmac path on the right, passing in front of the play area. Continue along it and keep left, descending to the riverside in Flatts Wood and the footbridge across the river. Don't cross this; stay on the north bank of the river and walk upstream to a footbridge over Percy Beck. Cross this and keep left, heading upstream alongside the river through the woods and ignoring any paths heading off to the right uphill. Keep an eye open for the remains of the once-impressive Tees Viaduct, which carried the old Darlington to Tebay railway high above the river; this was demolished in the 1960s when the line was closed. Keep on to reach a pair of moss-covered stones either side of the path, called the 'Wishing Stones'. Pass between them and climb some stone steps beside the river. Continue ahead through the woods to reach a gate in a stone wall (1).

Go through the gate and keep alongside the wall on your right to a gate. Go right through it and climb steeply uphill through trees to a fence/gate at the top. Go through the gate into a field, and turn right alongside the fence. Follow this over several fields to reach the line of the old railway. Cross this and keep on alongside the fence until you reach a footpath sign. Go right here back into the woods and follow the path downhill, keeping left at the forks to reach a footbridge over Percy Beck. Cross this and go right uphill to exit the woods onto Raby Av. Continue along this

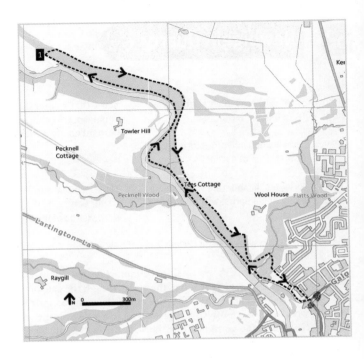

to the T-junction at the end. Go left and then right onto Flatts Rd, which leads back to Scar Top.

Points of interest

Flatts Wood by the river is a remnant of the Marwood Chase hunting forest. Lord Barnard (Raby Estates) owns some of Flatts Wood, and Durham County Council the rest. Raby have recently felled part of the woods and are replanting with oak and beech. Other areas replanted about twenty years ago are larch, oak and beech. Deer, squirrels and other animals live in the woods.

The popular Rock Walk was created more than 100 years ago by Dr George Edwards, who first had to get permission from the Earl of Darlington. It is one of three well-known walks in Flatts Wood.

Newbiggin Quarry

START Bowlees Visitor Centre, DL12 0XF, GR NY907282

DISTANCE 4¼ miles/6.8km with 600ft/180m of ascent

SUMMARY A moderate walk mainly along fields paths, with some road walking

MAPS OS Explorer OL31 North Pennines; OS Landranger 92 Barnard Castle & Richmond

PARKING Park and donate parking

WHERE TO EAT AND DRINK Bowlees Visitor Centre, T01833-622145, www.visitbowlees.org.uk

A pleasant walk around the environs of Bowlees and Newbiggin.

Leave the car park by crossing the footbridge over Bowlee Beck and go up the steps. At the top of these go through the gate on your right into the woods. Stay on this path as it follows the boundary wall of the woods, cross a footbridge and keep on to a stile over the wall on the left. Cross this and go right along the wall, through a gate, and keep on over rough grass to reach a stream (**1**).

Ford the stream and go through the gate ahead, climb the grassy bank to another gate, go through this and then continue diagonally left across the fields to Broadley's Gate. Go through the gate and follow the track around to the right of the buildings, staying on this to reach a minor road at Watson's Bridge. Go right along the road to a cattle grid at Moor House (**2**).

Cross the cattle grid and go into the farmyard, exiting through the gate in the right-hand wall. Go right along the edge of the field and continue to Red Grooves Gill. Cross the stream and keep right along the field edges for three more fields to join a track. Go right along this and follow it past the old quarry to reach a surfaced road (**3**).

Turn left along the road and then left downhill at the first junction. Keep on downhill along the road to pass through Newbiggin village. Ignore the roads leading off on the left, and continue on through the houses to where the road forks, keeping left uphill to a gate on the left. Leave the road here and follow the path across two fields to Hood Gill. Go right over a stile and then follow the wall on the left of the field to a gate. Go through this and keep straight ahead over the next field to a track. Turn left here and make your way back to the car park.

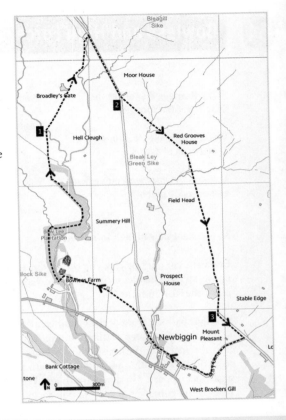

The village of Newbiggin dates back to the fourteenth century. However, no structures of medieval date survive within the surrounding landscape, and no medieval finds have been reported from the village. It may never have been more than a small group of timber-built houses, perhaps as a single farmstead, for several centuries. The village went through major development changes during the eighteenth and early nineteenth centuries, when fields surrounding the village were enclosed and many of today's buildings erected. These developments were, in part, associated with the growth of the local lead industry.

Bowless and High Force

START Bowlees Visitor Centre, DL12 0XF, GR NY907282

DISTANCE 4¼ miles/6.8km with 450ft/135m of ascent

SUMMARY An easy walk along field and riverside paths

MAPS OS Explorer OL31 North Pennines; OS Landranger 92 Barnard Castle & Richmond

PARKING Park and donate parking

WHERE TO EAT AND DRINK Bowlees Visitor Centre, T01833-622145, www.visitbowlees.org.uk

An excellent walk to High Force waterfall.

Leave the car park by crossing the footbridge over Bowlee Beck, and go up the steps to Bowlees Visitor Centre. Pass the building on your left to reach the road in front (**1**).

Go right past the front of the visitor centre onto the track leading uphill across the fields. Keep on this, passing Ash Hill to reach the hamlet of Dirt Pit. Just after the houses the road forks; go right and cross the road to a stile. Go over this and follow the path across the field, aiming for a gate near a barn. Go through this and keep straight ahead towards a black barn, going left in front of it to a gate. Go through this and follow the track downhill into the car park at High Force. Walk through the car park/picnic area to the High Force hotel (**2**).

After paying the entrance fee at the gift shop, cross the B6277 and go through the gate leading to High Force. It is a good track through the woods to the falls, with steps down onto the rocks at the end. After visiting the falls retrace your route back to the road (**2**).

Go right along the B6277 for a short distance and then go right on a path leading down through the woods; towards the bottom are steps leading to a gate. Go through this onto the banks of the River Tees again, turning left downstream along the edge of the field until you reach a footbridge across the river. Go right over the bridge to join the Pennine Way, and on the other side go left downstream heading for Low Force.

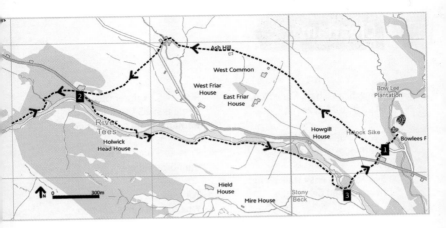

This section of the river has many smaller falls and rapids. It's a popular section for canoeists, so don't be surprised if you see any passing. Low Force is made up of a series of small falls covering a couple of hundred yards of the river; the middle set is the biggest. One of the nicest views of the falls is from the viewpoint beside the Wynch Bridge (3).

Cross the suspension bridge and follow the path up through the trees to a stile, cross this and continue across two fields to the B6277. Cross over and turn right and then immediately left along the lane leading back to the visitor centre (1).

Retrace your route back to the car park.

Points of interest

The dramatic High Force falls have been formed over thousands of years by the water wearing away the layers of shale and limestone from between the sections of harder volcanic Whin Sill.

START Scarth Hall, Staindrop,
DL2 3JL, GR NZ127205

DISTANCE 4¼ miles/6.8km with
260ft/8om of ascent

SUMMARY An easy walk along
riverside and field paths

MAPS OS Explorer OL31 North
Pennines; OS Landranger 92
Barnard Castle & Richmond

PARKING Roadside parking in
Staindrop village

WHERE TO EAT AND DRINK The
Wheatsheaf Inn, Staindrop,
T01833-660129

A walk over the fields between the villages of Staindrop and Cleatlam.

Go along the lane to the right of the village hall, and at the bottom of
this go right past buildings to a gate/stile into a field. Go diagonally left
across this field to another gate. Go through this and continue in the
same direction across more fields to a stile beside Cleatlam Bridge (1).

Cross the road and take the path on the northern side of Sudburn Beck;
this goes through several small fields to reach the A688. Go up steps and
cross the busy road, then through a kissing gate to continue alongside
Sudburn Beck to reach a footbridge across it (2).

Go left over the bridge and up steps to join a track. Follow this to the
A688 again, cross the road and go to the right to find a stile over the
fence. Cross this and go diagonally right over the field to another stile,
going over this and then following the fence along the left edge of the
field. Cross a double stile at the end and go diagonally right over three
fields to reach a gate beside a barn. Go through this and then left along
the road through Cleatlam village. Keep on the road to a footpath sign
on the left beside a gate/stile (3).

Go left over the stile and follow the track along the field edge, crossing
three fields to reach Sudburn Beck again. Go right, downstream, and
follow the beck back to Cleatlam Bridge. It is necessary to take a slight
detour to the right along the wall to cross a stile. Go left along the

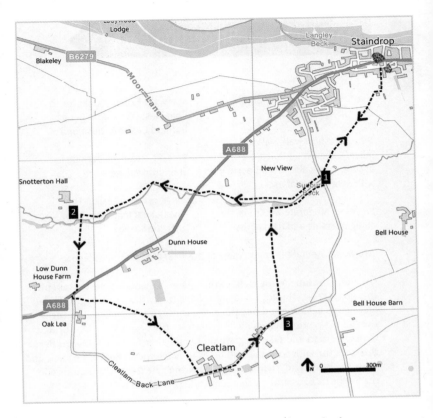

road back to the bridge, and then retrace your outward route back to Staindrop village.

Points of interest

Scarth Hall was built in 1875 in memory of Mr T. F. Scarth, land agent to the Dukes of Cleveland of Raby Castle. An upstairs room was added after the 1914–1918 war to commemorate the men from Staindrop who died in that conflict. During the Second World War, the Hall was used to provide NAAFI facilities to soldiers stationed in Staindrop.

Staindrop and Streatlam Park

START Scarth Hall, Staindrop, DL2 3JL , GR NZ127205

DISTANCE Short walk – 4½ miles/7.2km with 280ft/85m of ascent; long walk – 6¾ miles/10.9km with 430ft/130m of ascent

SUMMARY Moderate walks mainly along riverside and field paths

MAPS OS Explorer OL31 North Pennines; OS Landranger 92 Barnard Castle & Richmond

PARKING Roadside parking in Staindrop village

WHERE TO EAT AND DRINK The Wheatsheaf Inn, Staindrop, T01833-660129

Two walks around the countryside to the west of Staindrop village.

Go along the lane to the right of the village hall, and at the bottom of this go right past buildings to a gate/stile into a field. Go diagonally left across this field to another gate, going through this and continuing in the same direction across more fields to a stile beside Cleatlam Bridge. Cross the road and take the path on the northern side of Sudburn Beck; this goes through several small fields to reach the A688. Go up steps and cross the busy road, then through a kissing gate to continue alongside the Sudburn Beck and reach a footbridge across it (**1**).

Go right past Snotterton Hall and then right along the track. Where this starts to descend leave it and go left along another track over two fields to a ladder stile in the corner. Go right over this and head straight across fields to Scaife House. Go through the gate into the yard, go half right between the buildings, and follow the track to Moor La. Go right along the road and then left to reach West Lodge (**4**).

Go right in front of the building and follow the path alongside the Raby Park wall. Where the wall curves left, leave it and cross diagonally right across the field to a stile. Cross and follow a path over fields back into Staindrop village. Pass between houses and then go right onto the North Green. Cross the road and walk left back to Scarth Hall.

For the longer walk, at (**1**) keep straight ahead alongside the stream

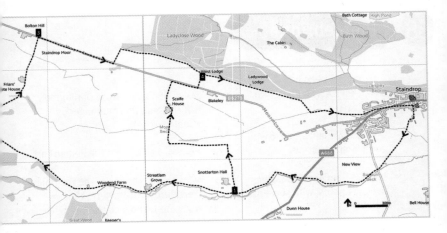

to reach Streatlam Grove, passing to the left of the buildings and continuing across fields to Woodend Farm. Pass between the cottage and farm buildings and keep straight ahead to the corner of a wall. Go right and walk alongside this to where it bears left. Go through a gate and go diagonally left across the field towards High House (**2**).

Just before the trees, go right through a gate onto a path, passing a disused quarry, and at the end of the wood cross a stile and go right along the field edge. After two fields go left towards Friar Cote. Continue along the track past the farm to reach Moor La (**3**). Go right along it for about ½ mile, then go left along a track. At the corner of the Raby Park wall, turn right along it and follow it to West Lodge (**4**).

Points of interest

Staindrop is one of County Durham's 'green villages', with mainly eighteenth-century stone houses surrounding a series of interlocking greens.

Piercebridge

START Piercebridge, DL2 3SJ, GR NZ211159

DISTANCE 4½ miles/7.2km with 200ft/60m of ascent

SUMMARY An easy walk along riverside paths, with some road walking

MAPS OS Explorer 304 Darlington & Richmond; OS Landranger 93 Middlesbrough

PARKING Lay-by near the Roman Fort

WHERE TO EAT AND DRINK The Fox Hole, Piercebridge, T01325-374286, www.the-foxhole.co.uk

A short walk between the villages of Piercebridge and Gainford.

From the lay-by go left, passing The Fox Hole pub, and continue to the A67. Turn left and walk along the grass verge; there is no path at first but one appears as you progress along the road. Keep along the path. After passing White Cross Farm the path crosses over to the other side of the road. Keep along this; in places the path becomes sections of the old A67 before it was widened. After crossing a bridge over an old railway – a branch line that used to go to a quarry near Fawcett village – the road joins the A67 **(1)**.

A short diversion along the road into Gainford village can be made here by going right along the A67. The village has a pleasant village green, church and a number of cafés/tea rooms.

Cross the road here, and go through the gate ahead into a field, following the fenced path left across this to reach an archway under the railway line that was crossed earlier. Go under this and ahead over the field beyond. Keep along the fence on the right of the field and follow this through several more fields, heading back towards Piercebridge and passing the imposing Snow Hall, which sits high on an outcrop to your left. There are glimpses of the River Tees below to your right through the trees, but access to the riverside path is private. Pass an arched bridge carrying two water pipes over the River Tees, built in 1936.

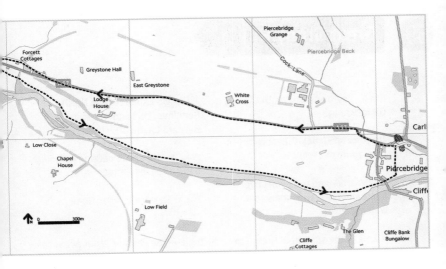

About half a mile or so after the bridge you will come to the outskirts of Piercebridge village. Go right through a gate and walk along a track in front of a house, and on to some garages, going left in front of these and over stiles to the road. Cross the road, down some steps and then right to an archway beside a pink house. Go left under this and then keep left along a wall, which will lead you to the remains of the Roman Fort. Keep straight along the wall to a stile, crossing this to reach the car park.

Points of interest

Piercebridge Roman Fort (possibly originally known as Morbium or Vinovium) is a scheduled ancient monument situated in the village of Piercebridge on the banks of the River Tees. Romans were here from about AD70 until at least the early fifth century. There was an associated vicus and bathhouse at Piercebridge, and another vicus and a villa south of the river at Cliffe, Richmondshire. The Victorians used carved stones from this site when they built St Mary's church at Gainford.

Great Stony Hill

START Lay-by on B6277, DL12 0XX, GR NY827332

DISTANCE 5½ miles/8.8km with 970 feet/290m of ascent

SUMMARY A moderate walk over heather moors, with some road walking

MAPS OS Explorer OL31 North Pennines; OS Landranger 92 Barnard Castle & Richmond

PARKING Roadside parking just before Peases Cottage

WHERE TO EAT AND DRINK None

A walk to the summit of Great Stony Hill high on the Pennine Moor between Teesdale and Weardale.

From the lay-by walk along the B6277 for about a mile to Trough Gill. There are lovely views of the Harwood valley down to the left, which you will walk back through later in the walk **(1)**.

Go right through the gate into Trough Gill and head upstream. It will be necessary to cross the stream a few times where the banks have been eroded or have collapsed and blocked the path. The going gets easier when a sheepfold is reached. From here follow a faint path through the grass, which follows the line of old mine workings. Eventually you will reach a vehicle track. Go straight across this and keep on over the moor to a wire fence, going left along this to reach the trig point on Great Stony Hill. The views over the North Pennines are stunning from here **(2)**.

Leave the summit by heading south-east over pathless moors to reach the vehicle track again. Go right along this and follow it downhill to the B6277. Cross the road and go downhill over a rough pasture to cross Ashgill Beck via a footbridge. Continue over the rough pasture, ignore the footpath sign on the left and keep outside the wall on the open access land to reach a rough track **(3)**.

Go left along the track, which soon becomes surfaced, and follow it along the valley floor, passing several white farm buildings. The road

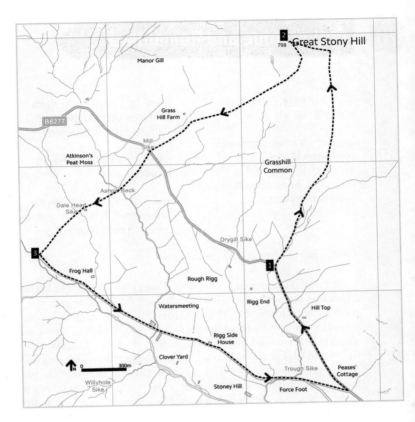

will eventually begin the climb up from the valley to the B6277. Where it forks, keep left to return to the main road and the lay-by.

Points of interest

Herdship nestles in the Harwood valley at the head of Teesdale, as bleak as it is beautiful. Here you can find some of the richest grasslands in the country; when spring arrives, it bursts into life. From a distance it looks like any other farmland, but take a closer look and it is farmland with a difference – a rich, man-made habitat, bursting with wild flowers and birds.

Cotherstone and Romaldkirk

START The Hagg, Cotherstone,
DL12 9QE, GR NZ011200

DISTANCE 5¾ miles/9.2km with
650ft/195m of ascent

SUMMARY A moderate walk on field
and riverside paths

MAPS OS Explorer OL31 North
Pennines; OS Landranger 92
Barnard Castle & Richmond

PARKING Parking area next to
recreation area

WHERE TO EAT AND DRINK The Red Lion,
Cotherstone, T01833-650236, www.
theredlionhotel.blogspot.com

A walk along two loops of the Teesdale Way.

From the parking area go left along the lane to the river. At the bottom
go left over the footbridge and keep following the riverside path to
reach a second footbridge (1). Don't cross this one; keep on the south
side of the river and walk upstream until rocky outcrops block the way
alongside the river. Go over the stile on the left into a field and follow the
right-hand edge of this to another stile, crossing this and keeping on to
reach a bridge over Wilden Beck. Immediately after crossing this, go left
into the field and then diagonally left across it. Pass to the right of a wall
along a track to reach the buildings at Woden Croft. Turn right in front
of the houses, and then keep to the right of the barn to enter the field
behind. Keep on alongside the wall until a gate on the right gives access
to a wooded area. Go through the gate and follow the path through the
woods. Exit via a gate close to the abandoned farm at Low Garth (2).

Pass to the left of the buildings to join a track, and follow this for a
short distance. Where it makes a sharp left turn, go right to a gate in the
hedge, diagonally crossing two fields to reach a gate which gives access
onto a walled lane. Go through the gate and along the lane, which will
bring you out onto the village green at Romaldkirk. Walk towards the
church and take the road off to the right, following this past the houses
to the far end of the green. Go left onto a footpath to a bridge over Beer
Beck. Cross this and, shortly after, cross a stile into a field, go diagonally
right across it to another stile, then go right following the path alongside

the wall edge over the next two fields to reach a road. Turn right and walk along the road to cross the River Tees over Egglestone Bridge (3).

Go right along the track and follow this to reach Jubilee Steps on the left, which lead up through the woods to reach the gate at the top. Exit the woods through the gate, aiming directly for East Barnley Farm across the next two fields. Keep left of the farm buildings to reach a gate (4).

Keep right along the wall across the next field to a gate. There is no discernible path across the next field; aim for the top of a tree visible on the horizon until a stile across the fence can be seen. Cross this and the field beyond to reach a stile through a wall. Cross this, go straight ahead to reach a fence, keep right and follow the fence line down to the edge of Shipley Wood. Keep alongside the wood until just after crossing a stream, then go over the stile on the right and follow the stream through the woods. Exit the woods via another stile and continue in the same direction to a caravan park. Pass beside a caravan and go directly across to reach a wooden gate. Go through this onto a track which leads down through the woods to reach the river. Go right to a footbridge over the river to (1), then turn left and follow the path back to the car park.

Forest-in-Teesdale

START High Force car park, DL12 0XH, GR NY885286

DISTANCE 5¾ miles/9.2km with 605ft/185m of ascent

SUMMARY An easy walk along field/riverside paths

MAPS OS Explorer OL31 North Pennines; OS Landranger 92 Barnard Castle & Richmond

PARKING Pay and display car park beside hotel

WHERE TO EAT AND DRINK High Force Hotel, T01833-622336, www.thehighforcehotel.co.uk

A walk through Upper Teesdale with great panoramic views of the dale.

From the car park go right along the B6277 to the entrance to the quarry. Turn left down the access road as far as the track leading to East Force Garth. Go right along this and pass to the left of the buildings, continuing along the track to a gate (**1**).

Go through this and leave the track, going left over rough grass and following the wall on the left side of the pasture to a gate in the far corner. Go through this, then go diagonally left down across the field to a stile in the wall on the right. Cross and walk towards the buildings at Hill End, passing to the right of these to join a track. Go right along this, to a concrete track, then go left and follow this to the bridge over the River Tees. Don't cross it; go right upstream along the banks of the River Tees to Saur Hill Bridge (**2**).

Here, go right uphill along a track to a gate in the wall on the left. Go through this and keep on the track, passing New House to reach the B6277. Cross, and go up the track directly ahead, going right after passing the first wall. Continue along this path, which crosses several pastures, before joining a walled lane near Gillet House. Pass behind this and keep on to reach the road in Forest-in-Teesdale opposite the village school. Go left and pass behind the school, then keep on the road to the end where a stile gives access onto fields. Continue in the same direction across three fields to reach a minor road (**3**).

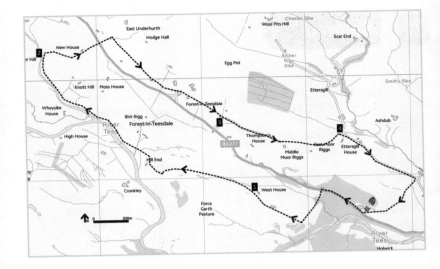

Go left along this and follow it to Middle Moor Riggs. Here, go left onto a grassy track along the right-hand wall of the field, and after four fields go left downhill to reach another minor road beside a cottage **(4)**.

Go right along the road, following it to the road junction leading to Dirt Pit. Leave the road here and go right over a stile into a field, crossing this to a gate beside a barn. Go through the gate and continue ahead towards a black barn, turning left past this to another gate. Go through the gate and follow the track down to the car park at High Force.

Points of interest

Much of the second half of this walk is along the route of the original main road from Langdon Beck to Newbiggin via Dirt Pit, which was in regular use until the B6277 was built circa 1820.

Boldron

START Scar Top, Barnard Castle, DL12 8PW, GR NZ049166

DISTANCE 5¾ miles/9.2km with 550ft/165m of ascent

SUMMARY A moderate walk mainly on field/riverside paths

MAPS OS Explorer OL31 North Pennines; OS Landranger 92 Barnard Castle & Richmond

PARKING Various car parks available in Barnard Castle

WHERE TO EAT AND DRINK Various pubs/cafés in Barnard Castle

An interesting walk over the fields to the south of Barnard Castle.

From Scar Top, go right along Horse Market to the Butter Market. Keep on down The Bank until you are opposite the Blue Bell pub. Cross the road, go left past the pub and walk along Thorngate. At the end pass between buildings and cross over the footbridge. Go straight ahead from the footbridge, uphill, and where the path forks, go left to reach The Lendings. Go left along this to the end, then over a stile into the caravan park. Go right along the road, and then right over the cattle grid to exit it. Just after the cattle grid go left over a stile and follow the path over three fields to a minor road (**1**).

Go left along the road to Egglestone Abbey. At the road junction go left uphill to the abbey, and pass by this, heading for the farm buildings. Go left between the barns and continue to a gate, go through this, and then where the track forks go left to another gate. Go through this into a field and go right along the field edge, continuing along three fields to a track. Turn right here and then left through the hedge. Follow the fence on the right along the edge of a wood to stone gate posts, with Castle Farm over to your right. Here, go diagonally left across the field, cross a stream and continue in the same direction over the next field to the B6277 (**2**).

Cross the road and go to the right of a building, following the track towards the woods. Go over a stile on the left and continue to another stile, going right over this and across the field towards a barn. Pass to the right of the barn to a gate, go through this and continue straight

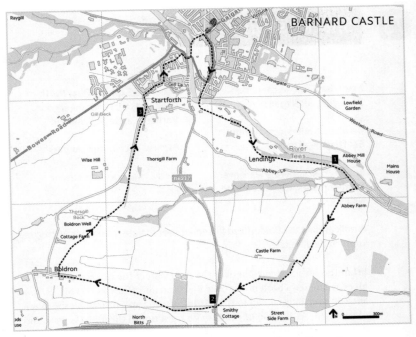

ahead across several narrow fields towards Boldron village. Go to the
left of the cottage to join a track which leads to the village, and keep on
to a footpath sign on the right, next to a grassy area. Go between the
houses and then keep on over the field beyond towards Cottage Farm.
Just before the farm buildings go diagonally right across the fields to a
barn, and cross the stile to the left of this. Keep along the right field edge
to pass a well, then down to cross a footbridge in the field corner. Go
right along the stream, cross a stile, then go left across the field to a gate.
Go through this and follow the field edge down to a gate beside the road.
Don't go onto the road; keep on the path that parallels it to Startforth
Hall Farm and go through the stile to join the road (3).

Go right along the road, then left at the junction, keeping left at the next
junction onto Boldron La, and follow this through Startforth. At the
junction with Low Startforth Rd, go left along this to just before the A67,
then go right along an alley to reach the County Bridge. Cross over this,
then go left along the path under the castle walls and follow it back to
Scar Top.

START Balderhead car park,
DL12 9UX, GR NY928187

DISTANCE 6 miles/9.7km with
640ft/195m of ascent

SUMMARY A moderate walk over
heather moors, with some road
walking

MAPS OS Explorer OL31 North
Pennines; OS Landranger 92
Barnard Castle & Richmond

PARKING Picnic area car park

WHERE TO EAT AND DRINK None

A walk around the Balderhead Reservoir over remote moorlands, with great
views of Baldersdale.

From the car park go right over the dam wall of the reservoir, which
gives great views both down over Blackton and Hury Reservoirs to the
left and over Balderhead to the flat-topped summit of Shacklesborough
to the right. At the end of the dam go right uphill through the gate and
follow the track to Water Knott (1).

Go through the yard of what is now an outdoor centre and exit via
the gate at the far end. The quad bike track curves off to the left; keep
on this over grassy moorland, and as it approaches Caper Gill go off
to the left to avoid a wet section. It is possible to go directly across
here and rejoin the track further on, or keep on the track to avoid the
possibility of wet feet. The track continues along Galloway Rigg to reach
a sheepfold, where it turns right and climbs up onto the summit of
Shacklesborough (2).

There are fine views in all directions from the trig point and cairn. On
a clear day it is possible to see as far as the Lake District Fells in the
north-west and the Cleveland Hills over to the east. From the summit
head north and descend through the rocky area, and then aim directly
ahead for the corner of the wall where it crosses Bleagill Hearne. There
is no path and it's wet/boggy in places, but there are no great difficulties.
At the wall corner cross the stream/wall and follow the wall west to
White Hill. Again, the going is pathless and wet/boggy, but dry ground

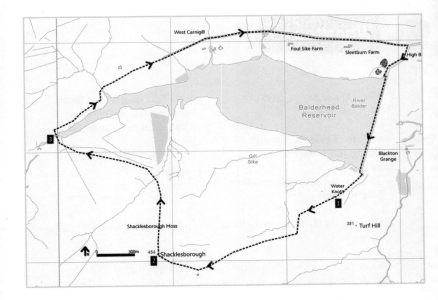

is reached in the form of a track leading to a shooting hut. Go right along this track to a gate in a stone wall (3).

Go through the gate and follow the track as it follows the edge of the reservoir around, cross Mea Sike, and continue to an open area where you will join a surfaced road. Keep ahead along the road and follow this back to the entrance of Balderhead Reservoir. Go right down the access road back to the car park.

Points of interest

Cotherstone Moor is a vast expanse of predominantly grassy moorland, punctuated by small, rocky and very distinctive flat-topped hills, of which Shacklesborough and Goldsborough are the most dramatic. This moorland rises up to the south of Baldersdale, and forms part of a much larger stretch of moorland that separates this tributary of Teesdale from Stainmore to the south. It is a wide, wild and windswept place.

Whorlton

START Abbey Bridge, DL12 9TN, GR NZ066148

DISTANCE 6 miles/9.7km with 430ft/130m of ascent

SUMMARY An easy walk mainly on field/riverside paths

MAPS OS Explorer OL31 North Pennines; OS Landranger 92 Barnard Castle & Richmond

PARKING Lay-by on the road to Egglestone Abbey

WHERE TO EAT AND DRINK None

A walk along the banks of the River Tees to Whorlton village from Egglestone Abbey.

From the lay-by walk along the road to the traffic lights on Abbey Bridge, cross the road and go along the path signposted on the right of the bridge through the woods. Follow this for about a mile till it meets a road, and go left to Dairy Bridge (1). Just before the bridge, where the road makes a sharp right turn, the 'Meeting of the Waters' can be seen down to the left.

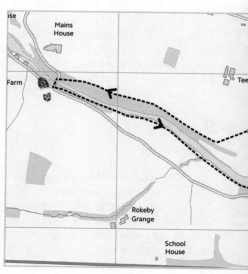

Cross the stile beside the gate and follow the track uphill towards Mortham Tower. Just before this the path goes left, passing a fenced enclosure to a stile over the wall. Cross this and keep along the right edge of three fields to reach a corner of a wood. Go left towards the wood and then pass to the right of it to a stone wall. Go right along the wall, passing a ruined building, to reach a gate in a facing wall. Go through this, then diagonally left across the field to a stile, which leads to Whorlton Bridge. Cross the suspension bridge and go up the steps behind the old toll cottage to reach the road at the top (2).

Go left along a path in front of a house and keep on this along the left edge of fields to reach a wooded ravine. Go down steps, cross a footbridge and climb up the steps at the other side to continue along the left edge of the fields. Eventually you will come to a gate beside the corner of the woods where the land falls away to the river (3).

Go through the gate and keep along the right edge of the field, heading towards a group of trees in the middle of the next field. Pass to the left of these to a stile over the wall. Go over this and cross the field to a gate in the far corner next to woods. Go right through the gate and walk along the edge of field/woods to a gate leading into the woods. Go left through it and follow the path, initially along the inside edge of the woods, then steeply down to join another path. Go right along this; it leads to the road at Abbey Bridge. Go left over the bridge, then right back to the start.

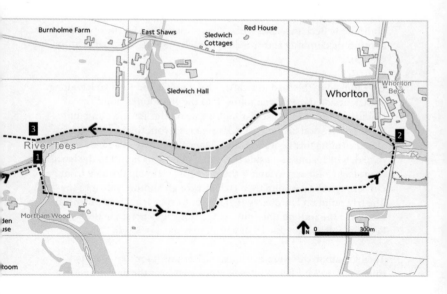

Hardberry Hill

START The drinking fountain, Middleton-in-Teesdale, DL12 0SH, GR NY947254

MAPS OS Explorer OL31 North Pennines; OS Landranger 92 Barnard Castle & Richmond

DISTANCE 6 miles/9.7km with 1,030ft/310m of ascent

PARKING Roadside parking in Middleton-in-Teesdale

SUMMARY A moderate walk mainly on field/moorland paths, with some road walking

WHERE TO EAT AND DRINK Various places in Middleton-in-Teesdale

An enjoyable walk over Hardberry Hill with grand views over Upper Teesdale.

From the drinking fountain go right along the Market Place towards the Middleton-in-Teesdale Hotel to the road junction outside it **(1)**. Go right uphill and walk along the road to where a road goes off to the left into woods. Go left along this and follow the road to where it ends near some old lime kilns **(2)**. Go left over the bridge and then keep right alongside Hudeshope Beck to Skears Beck. Cross this and go up the opposite bank, continuing climbing across fields to reach the Aukside road near to Club Gill **(3)**.

Go right along the road to a cattle grid, cross it and then go left along a track beside the wall and follow it to the abandoned buildings of Coldberry Mine. Here, go through a gate on the left and climb up through the spoil heaps, past a disused reservoir, then keep straight ahead, aiming for the wall in the distance. A grassy quad bike track is joined, which runs alongside the wall. Follow this uphill to the fence at the top of Coldberry Gutter – there are fine views up the dale from here. Go through the gate and then go left through another gate into the field. The trig point on Hardberry Hill is over to your left. Head downhill alongside the wall on the right. At the stone wall cross via the stile and keep on, following the wall downhill to reach a road **(4)**.

Turn left along this high level road and follow it for a couple of miles back to Middleton village – the views over the dale are superb

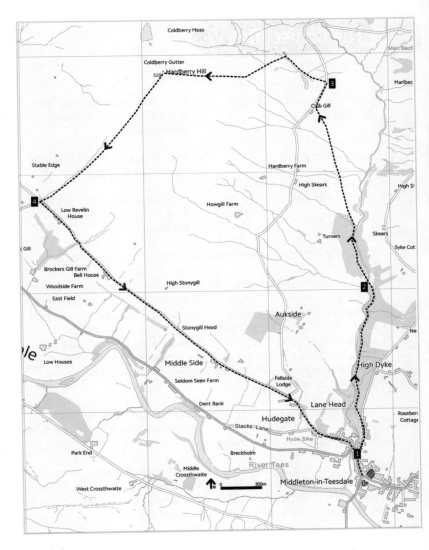

Coldberry Moss

Coldberry Gutter
Hardberry Hill

Stable Edge

Low Revelin House

Brockers Gill Farm
Bell House
Woodside Farm
East Field

Low Houses

Hardberry Farm

High Skears

Howgill Farm

Turners

High Stonygill

Stonygill Head

Middle Side

Seldom Seen Farm

Dent Bank

Hudegate

Stacks Lane

Breckholm

Middle Crossthwaite

West Crossthwaite

Club Gill

Skears

Syke Cot

Aukside

Fellside Lodge

Lane Head

High Dyke

Roseben Cottage

River Tees

Middleton-in-Teesdale

0   300m

100 Walks in County Durham

throughout. Ignore the turning on the left to Aukside and then, at the fork, keep left to pass the old London Lead Mining Company building to reach the B6277. Go left over the bridge, and then back through the Market Place to the drinking fountain.

The Coniscliffes

START Low Coniscliffe, DL2 2JX, GR NZ252141

DISTANCE 6 miles/9.7km with 200ft/60m of ascent

SUMMARY An easy walk along field and riverside paths

MAPS OS Explorer 304 Darlington & Richmond; OS Landranger 93 Middlesbrough

PARKING Lay-by on the A67 beside the Baydale Beck pub

WHERE TO EAT AND DRINK The Baydale Beck, T01325-469637, www. baydalebeck.co.uk

A figure-of-eight walk between the villages of High and Low Coniscliffe.

From the lay-by go left past the Baydale Beck pub and cross the road to a stile. Go over this and follow the path over fields into Low Coniscliffe village. Go left along the road, then left onto the Teesdale Way between houses to reach the riverside path. Cross a stile and follow the path upstream behind the houses. Walk through a parking area and keep along the river to pass under the A1 motorway. The path now hugs the river as it loops around under Manfield Scar to reach the ford to Swinelair Farm (1).

Stay on this side of the river and continue through mixed woodland along the river. Where the path exits the woods, keep left along the field edge to a footpath sign on the left (2).

Stay on the riverside path along the edge of a field, crossing a footbridge over Ulnaby Beck, then through an area of newly planted trees. The river now makes a lazy turn to High Coniscliffe. Just after passing the church, the path turns right and heads up into the village (3).

Go right along the A67, past the church and The Spotted Dog pub and head out of the village along the footpath. Just after crossing Ulnaby Beck cross the road and take the footpath left along the stream. Go left after going through the second hedge, then right after about 50m along a field edge to the footpath marker passed earlier (2).

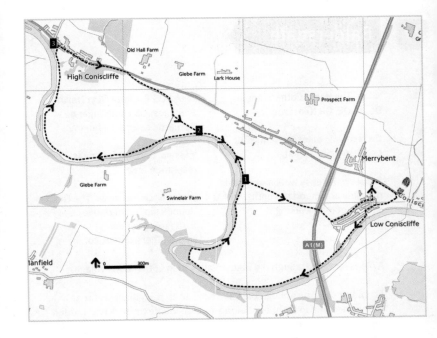

Retrace the route through woods back to (**1**). Go left, slightly uphill, and follow the track across fields to the bridge over the A1 motorway. Cross this and go left along the road after going through a gate. Walk along past the houses, and at the T-junction go left again to reach the A67. Cross the road and go right to get back to the lay-by.

Points of interest

The Saxon name for Coniscliffe was Ciningscliffe which means Kingscliffe. Edwin of Northumbria was the king and it is to him that the High Coniscliffe church is dedicated, the only church in England that is. The present church is thirteenth century but incorporates some Saxon stonework and a Norman door.

Baldersdale

START The Hagg, Cotherstone, DL12 9QE, GR NZ011200

DISTANCE 6½ miles/10.5km with 550ft/165m of ascent

SUMMARY An easy walk along field, riverside and moorland paths, with a section of road walking

MAPS OS Explorer OL31 North Pennines; OS Landranger 92 Barnard Castle & Richmond

PARKING Parking area near recreation area

WHERE TO EAT AND DRINK The Fox & Hounds Inn, Cotherstone, T01833-650241, www.cotherstonefox.co.uk

A pleasant walk through the Balder Valley from Cotherstone village.

From the parking area go back to the road to the village as far as a footpath sign. Go right here along a narrow lane to the River Balder, then go left upstream to the B6277. Go right over Balder Bridge and then left over a stile into the field. Go diagonally right across this and up into the trees to a gate. Go through this and follow the fence on the left through Doe Park caravan site. Stay alongside the fence across several meadows to reach the track bed of an old railway line; the impressive Balder Viaduct can be seen off to the left. Cross the railway line, then follow the overhead power line across the field to a gate. Go left through this onto a track, which leads to West End Farm **(1)**.

Enter the farmyard, go right between buildings and exit through a gate beside a barn. Go left across the field to a gate, and then follow more power lines across the field to an awkward stile across a stone wall. Continue over the fields beyond, aiming for a field barn in the distance. Cross a stile in front of this and then go diagonally left across the field, through gorse bushes and then steeply down to cross a footbridge. Then climb a steep grassy bank and follow a wall on the right to a barn, going through gates onto a walled lane, which leads to Lanquittes. Pass in front of the cottage, and follow the lane to a minor road below Hury Reservoir dam. Go left along the road, keeping left where it forks to reach Briscoe Farm. Go right at the road junction in front of the farm to a fork in the road **(2)**.

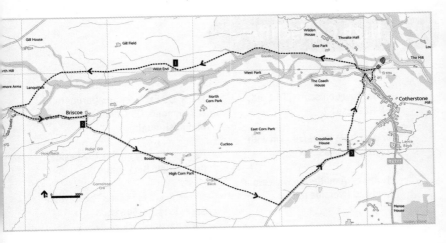

Go left at this fork and follow the unfenced road over the moorland to Booze Wood Farm. Leave the road where it turns to the farm and keep ahead along a grassy track over the moors to reach the Butter Stone. Go left along the road to Lance Bridge (3).

Go left here over a stile and follow the path across the fields to an old railway. Go straight across the track and then follow power lines down the field towards Cotherstone village. At the end of the field go over a stile onto a lane, go left and follow this to the B6277. Turn right and then left onto the lane leading down back to the car park.

Points of interest

The Butter Stone is an oddly shaped sandstone rock with a single cup mark. It takes its name from its role as a market point during the Great Plague of 1636, which badly affected the local villages. Town markets had been closed to reduce infection, and safe places to exchange goods were organized in isolated spots. Farm produce could be placed at the stone, and the seller retreated to a safe distance while the buyer took the goods and left coins in a bowl on the stone. The bowl was probably full of vinegar, to disinfect the coins.

High Coniscliffe

START Low Coniscliffe, DL2 2JX,
GR NZ252141

DISTANCE 6½ miles/10.5km with
235ft/70m of ascent

SUMMARY A moderate walk along
field and riverside paths

MAPS OS Explorer 304 Darlington
& Richmond; OS Landranger 93
Middlesbrough

PARKING Lay-by on the A67 beside
the Baydale Beck pub

WHERE TO EAT AND DRINK The Baydale
Beck, T01325-469637,
www.baydalebeck.co.uk

A circular walk between the villages of Low and High Coniscliffe.

From the lay-by go left past the Baydale Beck pub and cross the road to
a stile. Go over this and follow the path over fields into Low Coniscliffe
village. Go left along the road, then left onto the Teesdale Way between
houses to reach the riverside path. Cross a stile and follow the path
upstream behind the houses. Walk through a parking area and keep
along the river to pass under the A1 motorway. The path now hugs
the river as it loops around under Manfield Scar to reach the ford to
Swinelair Farm (1).

Stay on this side of the river and continue through mixed woodland
along the river. Where the path exits the woods, keep left along the field
edge to cross a footbridge over Ulnaby Beck, then continue through an
area of newly planted trees. The river now makes a lazy turn to High
Coniscliffe; just after passing the church, the path turns right and heads
up into the village (2).

Go right along the A67, past the church and The Spotted Dog pub, then
go left along Mill La, passing to the right of the house at the bottom
to cross over Ulnaby Beck. Go left upstream and follow it to another
footbridge beside a gate. Go right from the footbridge along a grassy
track, through a gate, keeping ahead along the field edge to cross a stile
over a fence. Keep to the same direction across the meadow to another

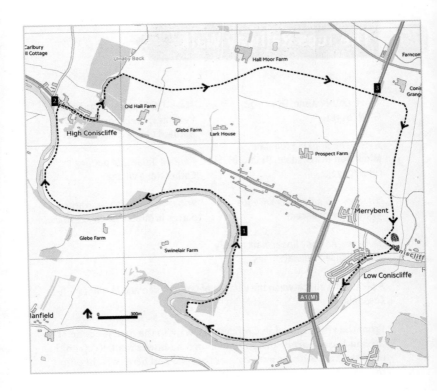

stile, cross this and cross next to two fields along the left edge. Cross a stile into a field and go diagonally left over this towards Hall Moor Farm. At the other side, go right through a gap in the hedge onto a lane. Go left along this, then right at the end over a stile, keeping diagonally left over the next field to a stile into woods in the far corner. Go through the woods, exiting over a stile, keeping left along the field edge to a stile on the left. Cross this, go right along the track, and follow it to cross over the A1 motorway (3).

Go right into a field, keeping along the left edge to join a track in front of Coniscliffe Grange. Go right along this track, continuing downhill over fields. Just after crossing a stream, the track forks. Keep right along a quiet lane, hedged on both sides, to return to the lay-by.

The Tees Railway Walk

START Cotherstone, DL12 9QB, GR NZ013194

FINISH The drinking fountain, Middleton-in-Teesdale, DL12 0SH, GR NY947254

DISTANCE 6½ miles/10.5km with 375ft/110m of ascent

SUMMARY An easy linear walk mainly along disused railways lines

MAPS OS Explorer OL31 North Pennines; OS Landranger 92 Barnard Castle & Richmond

PARKING Roadside parking in Cotherstone village

WHERE TO EAT AND DRINK Various places in Middleton-in-Teesdale

A pleasant walk between the villages of Cotherstone and Middleton-in-Teesdale.

From the village green in Cotherstone, walk to the road junction at the south-east corner and go right along the Bowes road. Keep on this until the Tees Railway path crosses the road and here go right onto the track bed of the old railway. It's easy walking along the old track

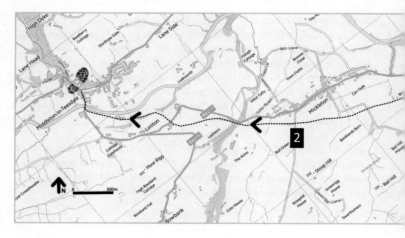

bed, so you can enjoy the views of the River Tees valley. Keep on until you come to the Baldersdale road, and cross this to shortly reach the Baldersdale viaduct. This is one of two of the old viaducts that you will cross on the walk; both are impressive structures and give great views, and were lucky to survive the demolition teams when the line was closed in 1964. Keep on heading north, cross another minor road, and then when you reach the Romaldkirk road you have to briefly leave the line of the old railway. Go right along the road and walk into Romaldkirk, keeping left at the road junction into the village (1).

At the crossroads go left and walk along the lane past houses to where there is access again onto the old railway line. Turn right and continue along the track bed. Keep on for a couple of miles, cross another road, and continue through the car park close to Mickleton village, shortly after which you will come to another road (2).

Cross this and shortly afterwards you will come to the second of the viaducts, which spans the River Lune. Cross this and continue for about ¾ mile to Lonton. Here, the access along the old track bed stops. Exit right over a stile and cross the paddock to the B6277, then go left along this for a short distance to a stile on the right. Cross this and follow the path over fields to rejoin the road opposite the cattle market just outside Middleton. Go right along the road, cross the County Bridge and then continue along Bridge St into the village and the drinking fountain.

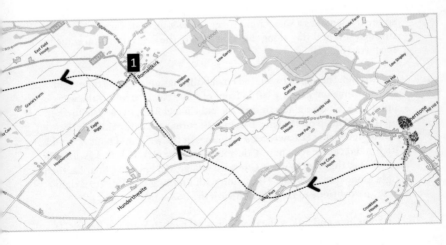

START Lay-by on A67, DL2 3QG,
GR NZ147171

DISTANCE 6½ miles/10.9km with
530ft/160m of ascent

SUMMARY An easy walk along field
and riverside path

MAPS OS Explorer 304 Darlington
& Richmond; OS Landranger 93
Middlesbrough

PARKING Lay-by on the A67 to the
east of Winston village

WHERE TO EAT AND DRINK The
Bridgewater Arms, Winston,
T01325-730302

An interesting walk to see the ruins of Old Richmond.

From the eastern end of the old section of road, go right through a gap
in the hedge and follow a track down to the banks of the River Tees.
Go right upstream and follow a good track behind the water treatment
works to reach the splendid Winston Bridge (1).

Cross this, go left through a gate and cross the field to some cottages,
where you will join a bridleway. Go left along this, crossing a stone
bridge and keeping along the left edge of the fields. After about a mile or
so the track makes a sharp right turn; follow it to a gate on the left. Go
through this and stay along the right edge of the fields until you come to
Barforth Hall (2).

Go through the gap between the farm buildings onto a lane, turn right
and continue on, keeping left in front of some barns to follow the way
uphill. Go left over a new bridge; the old Chapel Bridge is a little further
up the gill. Keep on the lane, passing the ruins of the tiny thirteenth-
century chapel of St Lawrence's. The lines of the walls and houses of Old
Richmond can be seen here. Continue along the elevated track, with fine
views over the river towards Gainford village. On reaching Boat La, turn
right along it to reach the T-junction with Pudding Hill Rd. Turn right
here and continue to the junction with the B6274 (3).

Go right here and follow the road downhill back to Winston Bridge (1).

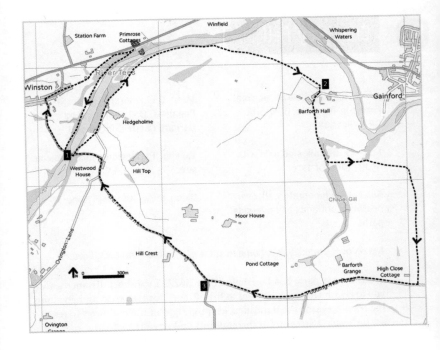

Here, you have a choice either to retrace your outward route back along the river, or alternatively keep on up the road into Winston village. At the T-junction go right, pass the village hall and then keep right along to the church. Enter the churchyard and pass to the left of the church along a footpath, which will take you down to the A67. Turn right back to the lay-by.

Points of interest

Boat Lane is so named because in years gone by there was a regular ferry service operating from its northern end, over the River Tees to Gainford on the opposite bank.

Cronkley Fell

START Hangingshaw picnic area, Forest-in-Teesdale, DL12 0HA, GR NY867298

DISTANCE 6¾ miles/10.9km with 850ft/260m of ascent

SUMMARY A moderate walk over heather moorlands and riverside paths

MAPS OS Explorer OL31 North Pennines; OS Landranger 92 Barnard Castle & Richmond

PARKING Parking area next to picnic site

WHERE TO EAT AND DRINK None

A walk over Cronkley Fell, home to some of Britain's rarest wildflowers.

From the car park, head west along the B6277 for a short distance until you arrive at the track leading to Birk Rigg. Cross the road and go along the track towards the buildings, keeping right of the buildings to reach a stile beside a stream. Go through this and cross the pasture, keeping left of the barn, and then go right through two gates. After the second gate go left downhill and across a boggy section to reach a track. Join the track and walk towards the bridge over the River Tees (**1**).

Keep left along the track towards Cronkley Farm; at the farm entrance the path goes right over a stile and behind the barn to reach the foot of a rocky outcrop. Follow the path up through the rocks, going right over a stile at the top, then left along a paved section heading for Bracken Rigg (**2**).

Turn right on Bracken Rigg and follow the path heading down to a gate in the corner. Go through this and continue in the same direction until you reach a broad grassy track. Go right and follow this as it climbs up Cronkley Fell. Eventually you will reach the first of several fenced enclosures; these are there to stop the sheep/rabbits from damaging rare alpine plants such as spring gentians and bird's-eye primroses that grow here. Continue over Cronkley Fell, passing more enclosures, until you come to White Well, a natural spring where crystal-clear water trickles out from the limestone rocks. There are great views here over Cow Green

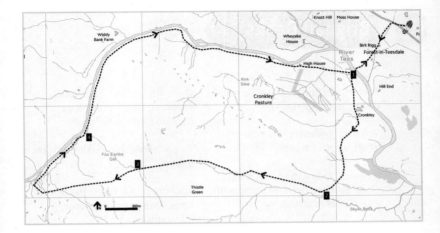

Reservoir, towards the distant Cross Fell and to the radar station on top of Great Dun Fell (3).

The path now becomes a little boggier as it makes its way to the large cairn at Man Gate, where the descent down to the river begins. At the bottom the path cuts across a very wet section before reaching the banks of the River Tees. Turn right and follow the river downstream to reach a gate (4); this marks the start of the awkward section beneath the slopes of Raven Scar. There's a bit of boulder hopping and some duck boards to negotiate. As you draw level with Widdybank Farm on the other side of the river, you will come to another gate and the walking becomes easier again. Continue downstream across several rough pastures until you arrive at a gate near a barn. Pass to the right of the barn and then keep right across the field, heading for a second barn where you join a track. Go left along this to reach a gate beside Cronkley Bridge. Cross this and retrace your outward route back to the car park.

Points of interest

Spring gentians are a very rare, alpine meadow wildflower confined to Teesdale in northern England and a handful of locations in western Ireland. They thrive on the sugar limestone outcrops on Widdybank Fell and Cronkley Fell.

Brignall Banks

START Greta Bridge, just off the A66, DL12 9SE, GR NZ085131

DISTANCE 7 miles/11.3km with 780ft/235m of ascent

SUMMARY A very strenuous walk along field and riverside paths, with a section of road walking

MAPS OS Explorer OL31 North Pennines; OS Landranger 92 Barnard Castle & Richmond

PARKING Roadside parking near the bridge

WHERE TO EAT AND DRINK The Morritt Arms, To1833-627232, www. themorritt.co.uk

A lovely walk through a gill immortalized by Sir Walter Scott.

Go over the stile beside Greta Bridge and cross the meadow beside the river. Walk through a wooded area to a metal gate. Go through this and keep along the left edge of the field to a stile on the left. Cross this and go down over rough pasture to a fingerpost, where you go left across a field to the ruins of St Mary's church. Pass to the right of these to re-enter woods, keeping ahead on the path through the trees to a wooden stile over a fence (1).

Cross the stile and keep on in the same direction to a hawthorn hedge. Go left down through the bushes into a riverside meadow. Keep straight ahead across this to a stile, which leads back into woods. Follow the path through the woods and onto the banks of the River Greta. In places the going underfoot is difficult. Eventually the path widens and the going becomes easier, the path climbing to a gate. Go through this, keeping left to join a road, then go left downhill along this to Brignall Mill. Go left in front of the house and follow the path around the left of the buildings to reach a footbridge over the River Greta (2).

Cross the bridge. The path goes briefly right, before curving back around to the left. Where it forks, keep left to reach the banks of the river again. Keep on downstream to cross a footbridge, go left after this and continue downstream. The going becomes difficult in places again, before a steep

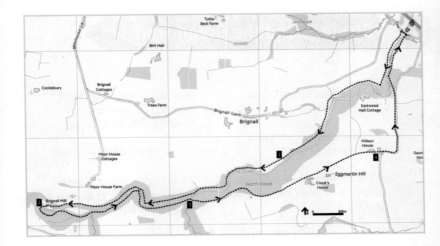

climb up Bank Scar. At the top of the climb, go left along a fence. The path widens through trees. Keep on to a fork in the path (3).

Go left downhill to ford a stream, followed by a steep climb back up the other side. The path now follows the edge of the woods high above the River Greta. Keep on following the fence line to reach a metal gate. Go through this, then left along the field edge to another gate beside a wooded area. Go through the gate and keep straight ahead to join a road. Go left along this and follow it to a junction just after Wilson House Farm (4).

Go left at this junction and follow the road downhill for about ½ mile to a footpath sign on the right. Leave the road and go left over a stile into the woods, then go right along the path steeply downhill through the trees. At the bottom exit the woods into a field, and keep straight ahead across this to pass between buildings onto a road. Go left over Greta Bridge back to the start.

WALK
83

Bowlees and the Green Trod

Start Bowlees Visitor Centre, DL12 0XF, GR NY907282

Distance 7 miles/11.3km with 730ft/220m of ascent

Summary A moderate walk over heather moorlands and riverside paths

Maps OS Explorer OL31 North Pennines; OS Landranger 92 Barnard Castle & Richmond

Parking Park and donate parking

Where to eat and drink Bowlees Visitor Centre, To1833-622145, www.visitbowlees.org.ukk

A walk over Holwick Moor, known as the Green Trod, visiting two of Teesdale's most famous landmarks.

From the car park, cross the footbridge over Bowlee Beck, heading for the Visitor Centre and passing through the yard to join a lane. Continue straight on, following the lane through the hamlet of Bowlees to reach the B6277. Cross the road and take the footpath signposted to Low Force, crossing two meadows. A gate/stile gives access to a wooded area, leading to the River Tees, the Wynch Bridge and Low Force (**1**).

Cross the bridge and take the path, heading away from the river towards Holwick village. Follow this path uphill across three meadows, to reach a road beside a cattle grid. Turn left and follow the road to reach Holwick village. At the T-junction, turn right and follow a track uphill, passing a house on the left. Keep left where is splits just after the house and continue uphill, passing through the impressive rocky outcrops of Holwick Scar to reach an ornate stile, featuring sheep and grouse sculptures (**2**).

Join a rough vehicle track and follow it for about a mile across Holwick Fell until a fingerpost on the left indicates the path leaving the track and heading across the sometimes

wet and boggy moorland. On this section of the walk over Whiteholme Bank to Skyer Beck, the path can be sketchy in places. Also two streams, Blea Beck and Skyer Beck, have to be crossed. Both have stepping stones, but after prolonged wet conditions these crossings can sometimes be problematic.

After crossing Skyer Beck, the path starts to climb up towards Cronkley Fell. Keep a look-out for a gate/sheepfold in the wall on the right (3), take a faint path through heather, and go through the gate to reach the Pennine Way on top of Bracken Rigg. Turn right and follow the path down through the juniper bushes, crossing two footbridges, and then continue across a flat meadow, passing the unsightly quarry works. The next footbridge is over Blea Beck, which you crossed earlier in the walk via stepping stones. A short detour along the beck to view the wonderful Bleabeck Force is well worth it.

Rejoin the Pennine Way and continue following the river downstream to reach the top of High Force. The best views of the falls are a few hundred metres downstream. Follow a path through juniper bushes, keeping an eye out for a path heading off on the left. Care is needed here as there are steep drops into the river below. Continue downstream again, following the River Tees about 2 miles back to Low Force. Ignore the green footbridge across the river (4) and keep on the south bank, with the river on one side and meadows on the other, to eventually reach Low Force and the Wynch Bridge again (1). Retrace the outward route back to the car park.

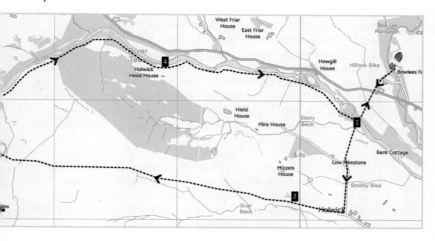

START Scar Top, Barnard Castle, DL12 8PW, GR NZ049166

DISTANCE 7 miles/11.3km with 590ft/180m of ascent

SUMMARY A moderate walk mainly on field/riverside paths

MAPS OS Explorer OL31 North Pennines; OS Landranger 92 Barnard Castle & Richmond

PARKING Various car parks available in Barnard Castle

WHERE TO EAT AND DRINK Various pubs/cafés in Barnard Castle

An interesting walk over the fields to Lartington, returning along the wooded Deepdale valley.

From Scar Top go right past the play area and then keep left, going downhill to join the path alongside the River Tees beside the footbridge. Cross the bridge (which gives great views of the castle) to the Lartington Rd, and go right along it until a footpath sign on the right. Take the track between the houses and follow it first across open meadows beside the river, and then into Pecknell Woods over a cattle grid. Continue on the track through the woods, passing a cottage on the right, until you reach a track going off on the left leading to a wooden gate. Follow this, through the gate and then across the meadow beyond, aiming for a cottage. Pass to the right of this to join a track, which leads to Pecknell Farm. Go straight through the farmyard in the same direction, exiting through a double set of metal gates. Then follow the path along the left-hand edge of the field to reach some buildings on the Lartington Estate. Keep along the field edge behind these to reach a gate, go left here onto a track and then right at the junction beside Dairy Cottage onto a road. Keep on the road to reach some more buildings, and go right where the road forks to enter Lartington village (1).

Go right along the B6277 through the village, which has many lovely cottages/houses, until it splits shortly after crossing the old railway line. Keep left along Lartington Green La, signposted to Bowes, and follow it as far as the track leading to Low Crag Farm. Go left along this through meadows. Where the track forks go right, passing through a small

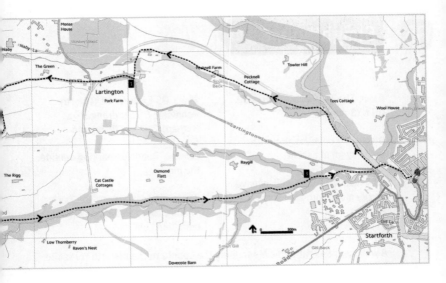

wooded area, and then over open meadows again, heading for Crag Pond. Keep on the track as it enters another wooded area. The pond is off to your right, but not visible because of the trees (2).

Shortly before reaching a stone wall, leave the track at the footpath marker on the left and follow the path through the trees. At first this is level, but soon drops down into the Deepdale valley – sections of this can be very wet and muddy, and care is needed. The return back through Deepdale is lovely despite the lack of any distant views because of the trees. The path undulates along the northern side of the valley, sometimes alongside the stream, other times high above it. Navigation is easy enough: there are two junctions where the path forks – each time keep to the left. The first time you will climb slightly to reach a seat and then go right past this. The second time you will go down along a sunken lane, which twists and turns to reach the footbridge over Raygill Beck. After crossing the footbridge, keep right to reach a surface track (3), go left along this to reach the B6277 Lartington Rd again. Cross this and walk a short distance to your left to reach the footbridge over the River Tees at the start of the walk. Go over it and then re-trace the outward route back to Scar Top.

Sleightholme

START The Tan Hill Inn, DL11 6ED, GR NY897066

DISTANCE 7 miles/11.3km with 580ft/175m of ascent

SUMMARY A difficult walk over wet boggy moorland, with some road walking

MAPS OS Explorer OL31 North Pennines; OS Landranger 92 Barnard Castle & Richmond

PARKING Roadside parking outside the inn

WHERE TO EAT AND DRINK The Tan Hill Inn, T01833-628246, www. tanhillinn.com

A walk over Sleightholme Moor along the County Durham/North Yorkshire border.

From the inn walk right along the road towards the cattle grid, cross the stile to the left of it, and follow the Pennine Way around the side of Clay Hill. The path over Sleightholme is waymarked using fenceposts painted white – don't confuse them with the smaller white sticks which mark the grit boxes that are used to put out medicated grit for the grouse – you could get lost! The first section of the path is relatively dry underfoot; however, it soon deteriorates and becomes wet and boggy. This walk isn't recommended after prolonged wet weather as sections of the path would probably become impassable. If you have any doubt about tackling the wet sections, it is better to turn back and have lunch at the inn. Keep on along the path, picking your way around the worst sections of bog to reach a large circular sheepfold (**1**).

Having reached the sheepfold, you are safe in the knowledge that the worst of the wet bits are behind you; it's still wet in places but nothing like what you've just tackled! Keep on following the path down alongside Frumming Beck, passing a large cairn beside the stream along the way. Ignore the first bridge you come to over the stream; the one you need is a little further downstream. You will join a vehicle track just before it. Turn right and follow the track over the bridge and keep along it until the junction with the Sleightholme Moor Rd (**2**).

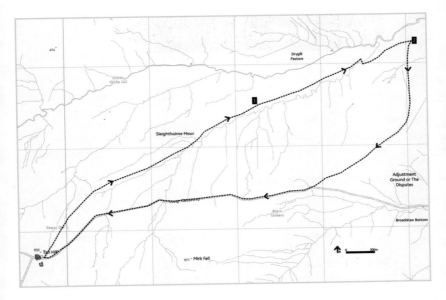

Turn right and follow the road over the heather moors. You can enjoy the views over flat moors now without having to worry about where you are putting your feet. You will see the traffic heading along the A66 away in the distance over Bowes Moor, with Mickle Fell, the highest point in County Durham, over to the north-west. Eventually you will come to the junction with a road leading to Tan Hill. Turn right and follow this back.

Points of interest

The Tan Hill Inn, at 1,732ft above sea level, claims the title of the highest pub in the country, and featured in Ted Moult's 1980s TV commercial for Everest double glazing.

Bowes and God's Bridge

START Bowes, DL2 9HU,
GR NY995135

DISTANCE 7½ miles/12km with
630ft/190m of ascent

SUMMARY A moderate walk over
heather moorlands and riverside
paths

MAPS OS Explorer OL31 North
Pennines; OS Landranger 92
Barnard Castle & Richmond

PARKING Small parking area opposite
the village hall

WHERE TO EAT AND DRINK None

A walk over Bowes Moor with superb views of the River Greta valley.

From the car park, head west straight along the main road through the village. Just after passing Dotheboys Hall, which features in Charles Dickens' novel, *Nicholas Nickleby*, turn right with the road to cross the A66 and climb up to Clint Top. There are good views over the Greta valley from here. Continue along the road for about 1½ miles to West Stoney Keld, passing through the remains of an old military storage site, where the foundations of many bunkers can still be seen **(1)**.

At West Stoney Keld go through a gate in the stone wall, then leave the Pennine Way by turning left and take a rough vehicle track heading south-west towards Ravock, at first following a wall on the left. Where this track makes a 90-degree turn to the right, go straight ahead to follow a faint path through heather, which is waymarked with posts and cairns **(2)**.

After about a mile you come to another wall. Turn right to follow it west to reach the other branch of the Bowes Loop on the Pennine Way, at Pasture End. Turn left and take the subway underneath the busy A66. It is then a short walk downhill to reach God's Bridge, a natural limestone bridge over the River Greta. The riverbed is usually dry, as is common with lots of rivers and streams in limestone areas; they run underground **(3)**.

At God's Bridge, go through the gate in the wall to find a new graded

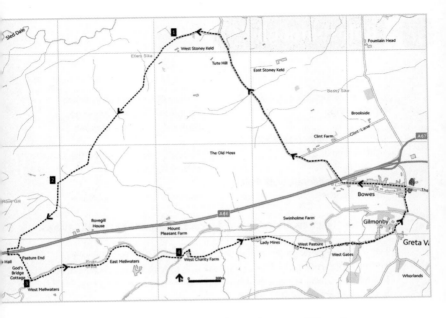

track through the fields (permissive path not shown on OS map). This takes you along the banks of the river, past East Mellwaters to a footbridge over Sleightholme Beck at West Charity (**4**).

After crossing the bridge, pass to the left of the farm, then go right through the yard. The track then turns left and heads through fields towards Lady Myres. Pass through the farm and continue on the track to reach a fingerpost. Turn left and head across a field to reach a footbridge over the River Greta. Cross the footbridge and climb to Swinholme to join the lane heading back towards Bowes. There are good views of the castle from here. On reaching a stile, cross a fence and instead of following the Pennine Way back into Bowes, follow the stream on the right through a field to reach the River Greta again. Turn left and take the path downstream to reach the lovely waterfall of Mill Force. From there, take the path heading diagonally uphill across a field to a walled lane, and follow it uphill to reach a lane close to the church. Turn right and follow this lane back to the car park.

Goldsborough

START Hury Reservoir, DL12 9UP, GR NY966192

DISTANCE 7½ miles/12km with 730ft/220m of ascent

SUMMARY A moderate walk mainly on good paths

MAPS OS Explorer OL31 North Pennines; OS Landranger 92 Barnard Castle & Richmond

PARKING Free car park on the south side of the dam

WHERE TO EAT AND DRINK None

An exhilarating walk around the Baldersdale valley, with outstanding views.

From the car park go left and cross the dam wall of Hury Reservoir, and go left through the gate on the far side to join a permissive path. Follow this along the north shore of the reservoir to reach a smaller dam between Blackton and Hury (**1**).

Go through the gate in the fence and keep to the north side of the pool to reach the dam of Blackton Reservoir; there are good views of Goldsborough from the water outlet tower. Keep following the permissive path along the north side of Blackton to reach the nature reserve at Birk Hat (**2**). This was the former home of Hannah Hauxwell, who used to farm in the valley.

Go right through a gate to join the access track, then go left along this uphill through Hannah's Meadows to reach the road. At the top go left along the road, as far as the entrance to Balderhead Reservoir. Here, go left downhill along the road and follow it over the impressive dam wall. At the far side, go left downhill along the track to Blackton Lodge. Go straight through the yard onto a track, which joins the Pennine Way near Blackton Bridge (**3**).

Go right along the track to where the Pennine Way splits; keep left and follow it over meadows to reach East Friar House. Go over the stile, and then immediately right to pass between a barn and wall to a gate. Go through this and then uphill along a track to a road. Go left along the road. Leave the road at the footpath marker on the right and follow a

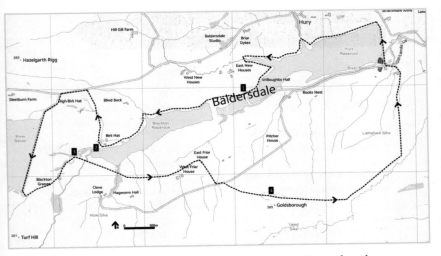

path uphill towards Goldsborough. Leave the Pennine Way path and
follow quad bike tracks up the grassy ramp between the rocky outcrops
to the summit of Goldsborough, which gives fine views over Baldersdale
and the surrounding countryside (**4**).

Leave the summit by following the quad bike tracks which head east
down over Goldsborough Rigg, continuing on to reach the steep-sided
valley of How Beck. Turn left here and follow the tracks alongside the
valley to just after crossing some wooden planks in the grass. Leave
the track here and head left over rough grass towards a gate in the wall
ahead. Go through the gate and cross the field to pass through another
gate. Then go left behind a barn onto the access track of West Briscoe
Farm. Go right down this to the road, then turn left back to the car
park.

Points of interest

Baldersdale is a secluded and beautiful valley, much of which was
flooded to create three reservoirs – Balderhead, Blackton and
Hury – built in the nineteenth century to supply water to Teesside.
The valley was home to Hannah Hauxwell, who shot to fame in the
1970s after TV programmes were made about her life.

Barnard Castle to Cotherstone

START Scar Top, Barnard Castle, DL12 8PW, GR NZ049166

DISTANCE 7½ miles/12km with 640ft/195m of ascent

SUMMARY A moderate walk mainly on field/riverside paths

MAPS OS Explorer OL31 North Pennines; OS Landranger 92 Barnard Castle & Richmond

PARKING Various car parks available in Barnard Castle

WHERE TO EAT AND DRINK Various pubs/cafés in Barnard Castle

An interesting walk, using two loops of the Teesdale Way path.

From Scar Top go right past the play area and then keep left, going downhill to join the path alongside the River Tees beside the footbridge **(1)**.

Don't cross this; keep on the north bank of the River Tees and follow the path upstream, crossing the footbridge over Percy Beck and keeping left along the River Tees. Continue for about a mile, ignoring any paths heading right, and stay along the river. Pass between two moss-covered rocks, the Wishing Stones, and then shortly after go up some stone steps beside the river. The path then turns left and continues to a gate on the edge of the woods. Go through this and keep along the right edge of the field to a second gate. Go through this and climb steeply through woods, exiting at the top through a gate into a field **(2)**.

Go left and keep alongside the fence, following the Teesdale Way, to pass East and West Holme Farms. Keep on in the same direction, along the edge of the wood/fields until Low Shipley Farm. Here, go left through a gate into the woods and follow the path downhill to reach the banks of the River Tees. Keep on over a grassy area to reach a footbridge over the river **(3)**.

Cross the footbridge and go left to reach a second bridge, cross this and then go right along a lane, keeping on it as it climbs to reach the B6277 in Cotherstone village. Go left and walk through the village to the

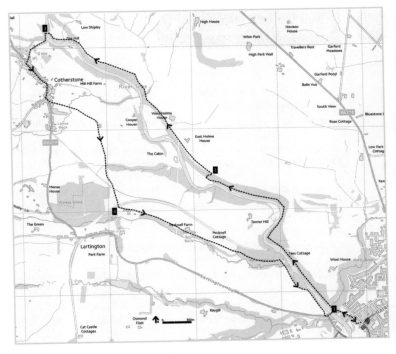

green, where the road forks to Bowes. Keep left on the B6277, and almost immediately go left along Mires La. Continue along the lane, and at the end go right over a stile, then along the fence to another stile. Cross this and go diagonally right across the next field towards the corner of a wood. Keep on in the same direction over more fields, cross two disused railway lines, the second via a tunnel, and just after this you will reach a gate on the left (4).

Go left through the gate and follow the right edge of the fields towards Pecknell Farm. Go through the gates and keep straight ahead through the yard onto a track, which leads to a cottage. Pass to the left of this and then continue across the field, to a gate on the far side. Go through the gate to shortly join a road in the woods. Go right along this and follow it firstly through the woods, and then after a cattle grid across fields to reach the B6277 Lartington Rd again. Go left and walk a short distance to your left to reach the footbridge over the River Tees, go over it and then retrace the outward route back to Scar Top.

Cauldron Snout

START Wheelsike car park, Cow Green Reservoir, DL12 0HX, GR NY811309

DISTANCE 7½ miles/12km with 720ft/220m of ascent

SUMMARY A difficult walk along roads and riverside paths, with a little scrambling

MAPS OS Explorer OL31 North Pennines; OS Landranger 92 Barnard Castle & Richmond

PARKING Small parking area beside the reservoir

WHERE TO EAT AND DRINK None

A walk around Widdybank Fell and along the River Tees to Cauldron Snout.

From the car park, turn left and walk back along the access road heading towards Langdon Beck. It's easy walking, all downhill, with great views over Upper Teesdale, but be mindful of the traffic. Keep right at the road junction and continue as far as the cattle grid beside the white barn (1).

Leave the road here and turn right onto a rough track heading to Widdybank Farm. This track winds its way across a couple of rough pastures towards the farm. During the spring months keep an eye out for the bird's-eye primroses – tiny little pink flowers – on the side of the track, especially around South Loom Sike. On reaching the farm, go through the yard, exiting through a gate onto open ground beyond (2).

The path now follows the banks of the River Tees through the rocky outcrops of Whin Sill. On the opposite bank you have Raven Scar on Cronkley Fell and you will pass underneath Falcon Clints on the slopes of Widdybank Fell a little further along. This does mean, however, that the conditions underfoot become a lot rockier as well. There are a few areas of boulders to be crossed – a little bit of time and patience is needed to cross these, plus a liberal use of the hands in places. Cauldron Snout can't be seen until the very last moment; you'll probably hear it first as you approach the confluence of the River Tees and Maize Beck. The climb up alongside the waterfall looks a little daunting from the bottom, but it's not that bad. There's a good route that climbs up through

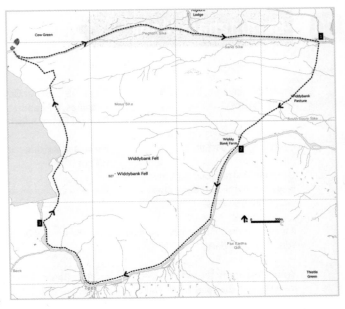

the rocks. The bottom bit is probably the hardest part, as there's a couple of sections where you will need hands and knees to get up the rocky steps. As you gain height the path levels off and you can enjoy the views of the water cascading down the falls. It's a very impressive sight, especially when there is a lot of water coming down them (**3**).

On reaching the road/bridge at the top of the falls, leave the Pennine Way, turning right to follow the road back over Widdybank Fell. Pass the huge concrete dam that holds back the waters of the River Tees to create the Cow Green Reservoir. There was a lot of dispute about its construction back in the 1970s as it destroyed large areas of rare flora. Follow the road past the weather station to reach a gate, go through this and turn left onto a track. Keep right where it forks and follow it back to the road. Go left and walk back to the car park.

Points of interest

The Cauldron Snout fall, which crashes down 200ft, is one of the most impressive waterfalls in Britain. From the top of the fall there are good views of Mickle Fell, the highest point in County Durham at 2,591ft.

Barningham Moor

START Barningham, DL11 7DN, GR NZ083102

DISTANCE 8 miles/13km with 920ft/275m of ascent

SUMMARY A strenuous walk along moorland paths that don't always match the OS maps!

MAPS OS Explorer OL31 North Pennines; OS Landranger 92 Barnard Castle & Richmond

PARKING Roadside parking in the village

WHERE TO EAT AND DRINK None

A walk over the heather-covered moors along the County Durham/North Yorkshire boundary.

Walk west along the main street through the village. Shortly after the houses stop, the road turns right. Leave it here and go left over a cattle grid onto a rough track over the open moors. Stay on this track until you reach a gate in a stone wall beside an old railway carriage (**1**).

Leave the track and go right onto the open moorland. There is a sketchy path, but navigation is easy. Follow the stone wall for the next couple of miles over the moors, so you can enjoy the views. Keep an eye out for some of the old boundary stones along the wall, Badger Way Stoop being the most prominent one. Just before the summit of How Tallon, there is a short steep section before reaching the trig point. Here, the wall stops, to be replaced by a wire fence. Keep on alongside the fence until you reach a metal gate (**2**).

Don't go through this; instead go right along the track away from the fence. This crosses the open moors to the head of Osmaril Gill with its outcrops of limestone, and continues around, heading towards the forest plantations in the distance. The paths on the ground don't match those on the OS maps; keep on the track until it takes a sharp left turn, leave it here and go right downhill steeply, heading roughly north and aiming for a gate in the fence on the edge of the plantation. Go down alongside a stream until a track heads off on the right; take this. You are aiming for the tarn in the distance. Some of the older OS maps don't show this, but

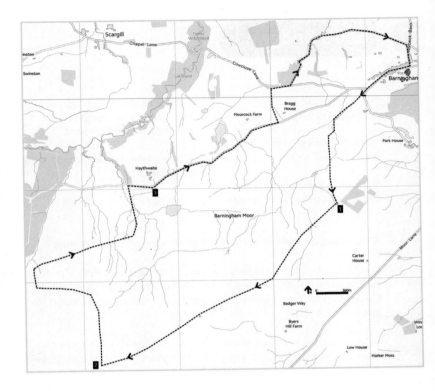

don't panic. Where the path forks, go left downhill to reach the corner of a wall. Keep left along the wall, crossing a stream, to reach a track at the bottom. Turn right along this to join a road at Haythwaite **(3)**.

Keep on this as far as Bragg House, then leave the road here by going left across rough grass to a walled lane. Go down this to join Cowclose La, turn right along it for a short distance, then left onto Low La. Pass an old lime kiln and keep on the walled lane, which can be wet in places, especially where a stream crosses its path. At the end of the lane is a set of crossroads; go right and walk along the road uphill back into Barningham village.

God's Bridge

START Bowes, DL2 9HU,
GR NY995135

DISTANCE 8 miles/13km with
650ft/195m of ascent

SUMMARY A moderate walk over
heather moorlands and riverside
paths

MAPS OS Explorer OL31 North
Pennines; OS Landranger 92
Barnard Castle & Richmond

PARKING Small parking area opposite
the village hall

WHERE TO EAT AND DRINK None

A walk along the River Greta valley to God's Bridge, with superb views.

From the car park go left along the road, cross Gilmonby Bridge and continue into Gilmonby itself. Just beyond the houses the road forks (**1**). Go right uphill and follow the road for about 4 miles over the moors to Sleightholme (**2**).

At Sleightholme join the Pennine Way and go right through a gate to cross two fields to Intake Bridge, over the stream. Cross this and climb the steep bank directly ahead, at the top going right along a wall and following this to a gate. Go through this and then right along a path through the heather to Trough Heads. Here, the Pennine Way splits. Go left over the heather moors until you reach a stone wall. Turn left and follow the wall to a stile on the right. Cross this and follow the path down to God's Bridge (**3**).

At God's Bridge, go through a gate in a wall to find a new graded track through the fields (permissive path not shown on OS map). This takes you along the banks of the river, past East Mellwaters, to a footbridge over Sleightholme Beck at West Charity (**4**).

After crossing the bridge, pass to the left of the farm, then go right through the yard. The track then turns left and heads through fields towards Lady Myres. Pass through the farm and continue on the track to reach a fingerpost. Turn left and head across the field to reach a footbridge over River Greta. Cross the footbridge and climb to

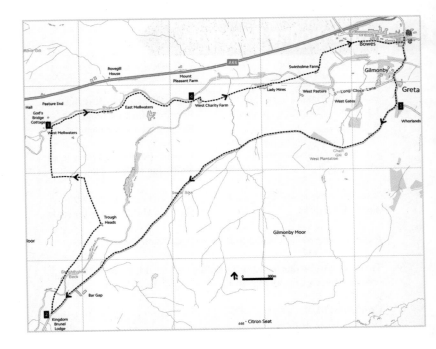

Swinholme to join the lane heading back towards Bowes. There are good views of the castle from here. On reaching a stile, cross the fence and follow the Pennine Way back into Bowes. On reaching the castle, go through the gate and go right along the road back to the car park.

Points of interest

Dotheboys Hall, in reality Bowes Academy, was the notorious school in Charles Dickens' novel *Nicholas Nickleby*. It was closed soon after Dickens visited in 1838. It was run by William Shaw and catered for about 100 boys.

Grassholme Reservoir

START The drinking fountain, Middleton-in-Teesdale, DL12 0SH, GR NY947254

MAPS OS Explorer OL31 North Pennines; OS Landranger 92 Barnard Castle & Richmond

DISTANCE 8 miles/13km with 1,040ft/315m of ascent

PARKING Roadside parking in Middleton-in-Teesdale

SUMMARY A moderate walk mainly along good tracks

WHERE TO EAT AND DRINK Various places in Middleton-in-Teesdale

An interesting walk from Middleton to Lunedale and back.

Turn left into Bridge St from the drinking fountain and go along it, crossing the County Bridge to reach the cattle market (**1**).

Continue uphill along the B6277. At the junction go right along the Holwick road, and then immediately left through a gate. Go steeply uphill along a rough track and continue alongside the wall to reach a gate. Just after the gate the track turns sharp left. Leave it at a cairn and follow the path over grass to another gate, go through this and keep on in the same direction, climbing over rough pastures to a gate in the wall. Go through this and continue along the Pennine Way over more pastures to a junction with a track beside a gate. Go left through the gate and continue downhill, passing Wythes Hill to reach the Lunedale road (**2**).

Cross this and continue along the Pennine Way down over pastures to Grassholme Farm. Pass this to reach another road, go left along it and follow it Grassholme Reservoir, on the 'new' bridge. When the water level in the reservoir is low sometimes the 'old' bridge can be seen in the pool on your right. Just after crossing the bridge, leave the road and go through the kissing gate on the left to join the permissive path along the south side of the reservoir. Follow this to reach the visitor centre, passing in front of it, and then go right uphill and follow the road out to the entrance. Go left along the minor road to the junction with the Swarthy Mere road (**3**).

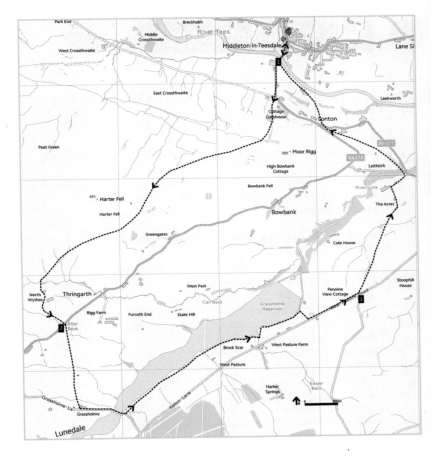

Leave the road and go left over a stile and go diagonally right over fields, crossing Eller Beck to reach a track. Go right along this to the track bed of the old railway line, now the Tees Valley Railway Walk. Go left along the disused railway, crossing the impressive Lunedale viaduct, and keep on to Lonton. Here, leave the disused line, go right over a stile, and cross the field to the road. Go left along the road for a short distance to a stile on the right, go over this and continue over fields back to the cattle market (1). Turn right and walk back into Middleton village.

High Acton, Hamsterley Forest

START The Grove, Hamsterley Forest,
DL13 3NL, GR NZ065298

DISTANCE 8¼ miles/13.3km with
1,200ft/365m of ascent

SUMMARY A moderate walk mainly
along forest tracks, which can be
muddy in places

MAPS OS Explorer OL31 North
Pennines; OS Landranger 92
Barnard Castle & Richmond

PARKING Pay and display parking

WHERE TO EAT AND DRINK Hamsterley
Forest Tearooms, T01388-488822
(open daily 10–5)

A walk through Hamsterley Forest, visiting some of the more remote sections
of the forest.

Exit the car park via the steps in the north-east corner, and follow
the path through the trees to a forest road. Cross this and go slightly
to your right onto another path through the trees. Follow this, going
down steps and across a grassy area to another forest road. Go left
along this, going over Euden Beck on a bridge. Pass some buildings
and keep on along the road, ignoring roads going off uphill on the
right and staying in the valley bottom. Continue on this road until
you cross Euden Beck again. About ½ mile afterwards, the road forks
(1).

Go left uphill here, and climb up onto Neighbour Moor. Continue along
the forest road, ignoring the road going off on the right, and keep on
the road until it crosses Acton Beck. Here, leave the road and take the
footpath going right uphill through the trees. Eventually you will come
to a T-junction of forest roads; go straight ahead along the road to the
edge of the forest at Ever Pools (2).

Go left downhill, following the track along the edge of the forest. At
the bottom, go left along the track. Follow this to the next junction,
then go right and keep along the road to Pennington Beech Wood. Go
right downhill, keeping right at the first junction, left at the second, and
continue downhill to where another forest road crosses. Here, go right
and follow the road down to the car park at Blackling Hole (3).

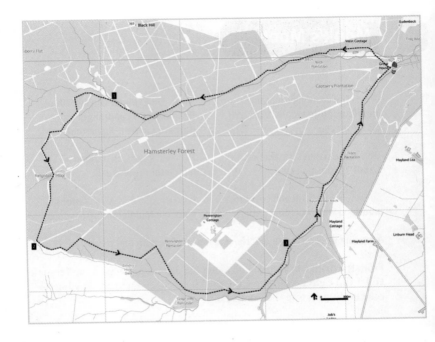

Go right over the bridge to join the forest drive. Go left along this and follow it back to The Grove.

START The drinking fountain, Middleton-in-Teesdale, DL12 0SH, GR NY947254

MAPS OS Explorer OL31 North Pennines; OS Landranger 92 Barnard Castle & Richmond

DISTANCE 8¼ miles/13.3km with 1,780ft/540m of ascent

PARKING Roadside parking in Middleton-in-Teesdale

SUMMARY A difficult walk over rough moorland with indistinct paths

WHERE TO EAT AND DRINK Various places in Middleton-in-Teesdale

A bracing walk on rough moorland and pastures, with fine views.

From the drinking fountain go along the market place, pass the Teesdale Hotel and right uphill where the road forks. Keep on to go left along a road leading off into the woods (1).

Almost immediately take the track going off to the right, keeping on this as it follows the edge of the woods into Snaisgill to reach a footbridge across a stream. Cross this and go up the steep bank in front of you to reach a path beside a wall, then go right along this to a gate. Go through the gate and turn right along the road, then left into a field. Cut across the left-hand corner of this to cross a stile into the next field. Go diagonally right uphill across this to a gate, and then continue in the same direction to reach a gate in the corner of the next field. Go through this and go left alongside the wall on a path, leaving the wall as the path turns uphill towards a cairn. Pass this and keep on the path to reach the summit of Monk's Moor (2).

Leave the summit by heading north-east; the path can be indistinct at times and the heather can make the walking difficult. Keep on to reach a gate/stile over the stone wall at the bottom. Cross this and go diagonally right down to some old mine buildings, where you join a track. Cross over the stream on the track and then go left, following the track to where the stream is re-crossed beside a gate/fence (3).

Go through the gate and keep left uphill, following a path. This runs parallel to the stream and passes old mine workings, eventually reaching a small tarn on the col. Pass to the right of this and go downhill on a rough track through spoil heaps to reach a minor road at the head of the Hudeshope valley. Go right along the road to a footpath marker on the left (4).

Go left over grass and follow the path over a stream, then keep on past mine buildings to reach a gate. Go through this and keep alongside the right-hand wall as far as a stile. Cross this and enter woods, then follow the path downhill to some old lime kilns where you join a road. Go left along this back to (1). Retrace your outward route back to the drinking fountain.

Points of interest

The miners' track that climbs from Great Eggleshope Beck over the shoulder of Monk's Moor was constructed by The London Lead Mining Company to carry traffic from the nearby mines.

WALK

95   Teesdale Waterfalls

START The drinking fountain, Middleton-in-Teesdale, DL12 0SH, GR NY947254

DISTANCE 8½ miles/13.7km with 850ft/255m of ascent

SUMMARY A moderate walk mainly on field/riverside paths, with some road walking

MAPS OS Explorer OL31 North Pennines; OS Landranger 92 Barnard Castle & Richmond

PARKING Roadside parking in Middleton-in-Teesdale

WHERE TO EAT AND DRINK Various places in Middleton-in-Teesdale

A walk visiting some of Teesdale waterfalls from Middleton-in-Teesdale.

From the drinking fountain go left along Bridge St, and follow this down over the County Bridge to join the Pennine Way. Go right along this between the telephone exchange and the cattle market. Keep on over fields and meadows to reach the footbridge over Eel Beck. Cross this and the stile beyond onto the banks of the River Tees. Go left, upstream (1), and continue to the arched wooden footbridge of Scoberry. Don't cross this; keep on following the river upstream to the next footbridge, the Wynch Bridge, a steel/wire suspension bridge across a rocky gorge. Low Force is a little upstream from here, although there is a good viewpoint of the falls from just beside the bridge. Cross over the bridge and follow the path through the trees up to a stile, crossing this and the two fields beyond to the B6277. Cross over to the right and then take the lane on the left leading to the Bowlees Visitor Centre. Go through the small yard to the right of this, then along the path leading to the car park, descending the steps and crossing the footbridge over Bowlee Beck (2).

Summerhill Force/Gibson's Cave are located ½ mile upstream from the car park. Go left after crossing the footbridge and follow the path through the old quarry and up the steps beside the first waterfall. Keep on to reach Summerhill Force, then retrace your route back to the car park. Exit the car park along the road to the B6277, cross and go right, and then left along the first track towards the farm. Pass through the yard and keep ahead to reach a footbridge on the left. Cross this and go

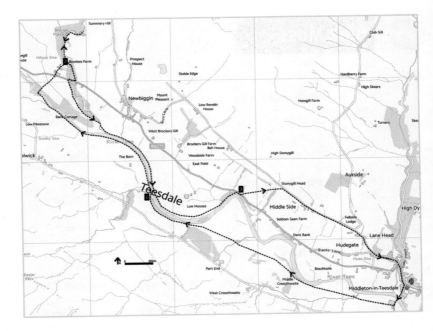

right and follow the stream down to its confluence with the Tees. Follow the riverside path along the banks of the Tees until you join the B6277 again (3).

Cross the road and go right to a footpath sign on the left. Go left through the gate and uphill across fields to reach a minor road at Stonygill Head. Turn right along this high level road and follow it back to Middleton village – the views over the dale are superb throughout. Ignore the turning on the left to Aukside. At the fork, keep left and pass the old London Lead Mining Company building to reach the B6277. Go left over the bridge, and then back through the Market Place to the drinking fountain.

Points of interest

Newbiggin's Methodist Chapel, built in 1759, is the oldest in Methodism. John Wesley preached here and services have been held continually ever since it was built.

Bink Moss

START Holwick, DL12 0NJ,
GR NY903270

DISTANCE 8½ miles/13.7km with
1,170ft/355m of ascent

SUMMARY A difficult walk mainly over
open moorland and tracks

MAPS OS Explorer OL31 North
Pennines; OS Landranger 92
Barnard Castle & Richmond

PARKING Roadside parking

WHERE TO EAT AND DRINK The
Strathmore Arms, Holwick,
T01833-640362,
www.strathmoregold.co.uk

A walk over the remote high moors between Lunedale and Teesdale.

From the parking area go left along a track towards a house; pass this
and where the track forks, keep left. When the track levels out, go
steeply down to the left to cross a stream, and then climb up through
the rocky outcrops to reach a gate. Go through this and continue
ahead to another gate. Keep straight ahead to reach a stream, cross
this and keep on to a second one. Cross this and go through a gate on
the other side, following the wall on the right uphill. The path will
then head left away from the wall over open moors to reach a gate
through a wall (1).

The next section over the high moorland between Teesdale and
Lunedale is very remote and rough going; it can be very wet underfoot
and exposed in bad weather, so go prepared! Go right along the wall,
climbing steeply up the bank, and then keep on along the wall/fence for
about 2½ miles to Bink Moss, the highest point of which is marked by a
wellington boot on top of a post. Keep on along the fence to Hagworm
Hill, where you join a footpath (2).

Go right, following the fence northwards as it starts to descend down
into Teesdale. After about a mile the footpath shown on the OS map
leaves the fence and heads towards Noon Hill. It is probably easier to
stay with the fence line and follow this down to some grouse butts and a
shooting hut, where you join a track (3).

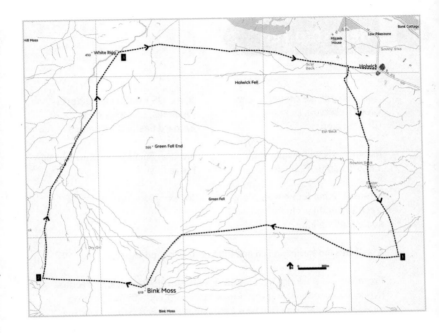

The difficult conditions are behind you now. Go right along the track, cross Blea Beck and follow the track over the moors back towards Holwick village. Where the track starts to descend and makes a sharp left turn, leave it and cross an ornate stile beside a gate. Continue along a track through Holwick Scars, which leads back to the village and the parking area.

Points of interest

Holwick consists of a few houses spread along a road in the pattern of a linear settlement.

Herdship Fell

START Wheelsike car park, Cow Green Reservoir, DL12 0HX, GR NY811309

DISTANCE 8¾ miles/14km with 1,450ft/440m of ascent

SUMMARY A moderate walk along track and pathless moorland, with some road walking

MAPS OS Explorer OL31 North Pennines; OS Landranger 92 Barnard Castle & Richmond

PARKING Small parking area beside the reservoir

WHERE TO EAT AND DRINK None

A walk around Herdship Fell and along the Harwood valley.

From the car park, go west along the rough vehicle track and follow this as it contours along the side of Herdship Fell. There are good views over the moors to Cross Fell, Great Dun Fell (with the white radar dome) and Meldon Fell on the other side of Cow Green Reservoir. After passing some old mine workings, the track turns and heads north to eventually join the B6277 (**1**).

You are now on the watershed between the Tyne and the Tees: any water running off the moor to the east will flow down into the Tees, while that going to the west goes into the South Tyne. Go right along the road and follow it to where it turns sharp left, leaving it here and going right downhill along Spitley Tongue into the Harwood valley. At the bottom of the valley the track becomes surfaced. Keep along it to a row of whitewashed cottages facing the road (**2**).

Go right here along a track down to the ruins of Harwood church, which sits in an idyllic position on the banks of the Harwood Beck. Cross the stream via the footbridge and go up through the gate into a rough pasture (*). Cross over this towards the barn, then pass to the right of it, going through a gate in the wall beyond into another rough pasture. Keep on in the same direction to the corner, and go through a hole in the wall onto open moorland. There is no visible path, but continue roughly due south to intersect the road near to a ruined building. Go right along the road and follow it back to the car park.

*Note that much of the next section of the walk is pathless over open moorlands. Good navigation skills would be needed in poor visibility. If you are in any doubt, after crossing the river

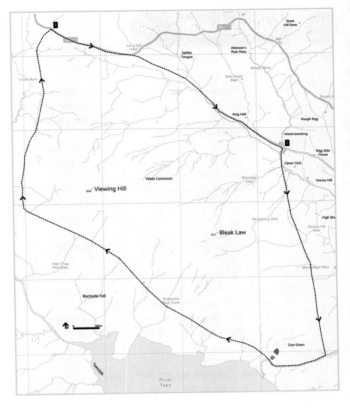

keep alongside the stream to reach Low End Bridge, go right along the road to the T-junction and then go right and follow the road back to the car park at Cow Green. It's about a mile longer but easier to follow in bad weather.

Points of interest

Cow Green Reservoir, approximately 2 miles (3km) long, was built between 1967 and 1971 to supply the industries of Teesside.

Holwick Fell

START Summerhouse, DL2 3UD, GR NZ202190

DISTANCE 9 miles/14.5km with 530ft/160m of ascent

SUMMARY A moderate walk mainly along narrow country lanes

MAPS OS Explorer 304 Darlington & Richmond; OS Landranger 93 Middlesbrough

PARKING Roadside parking beside the village green

WHERE TO EAT AND DRINK The Raby Hunt Inn, Summerhouse, T01325-374237

A pleasant walk around several small farming villages.

From the village green go north along the road to just after the houses. Here, go left through a gate and cross fields to reach the Killerby road. Go right along this into Killerby village, and continue through to where the road forks, keeping right onto Kiln La. Follow this to a T-junction, opposite a barn. Go right and follow the road to Morton Tinmouth village (1).

In Morton Tinmouth go left at the road junction, keeping along the road till it makes a sharp 90-degree turn. Leave it here and go left through a gate into a field, going right over this and three more to reach the road again beside the corner of a wood. Go left along the road into Hilton village, keeping left where the road forks to join the Ingleton road. Go left to Morley Moor House, then right in front of it, and follow the lane to a fork, keeping left and continuing to the crossroads with the B6279 (2).

Go straight over the crossroads onto Hulam La and stay on this heading towards Langton village. Keeping left where the lane forks, continue to a T-junction. Go right onto Ford Dike La, then left towards Headlam, keeping straight ahead to a T-junction. Go right and follow the road through Headlam to the entrance of Headlam Hall Hotel (3).

Go left through the gates, walk towards the hotel, pass to the left of it

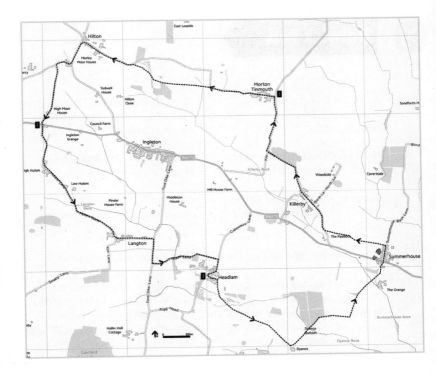

and go round right behind the building. Go through the car park and take the track on the left at the end over the golf course. Cross over Headlam Beck, go left along the field edge and follow this to where it makes a sharp 90-degree right turn. Go right, and where the hedge ends, go diagonally left across two fields to Dyance Farm. Go left onto a track behind the farm and follow this back to Summerhouse village.

Points of interest

The good views over distant Richmondshire and Teesdale, the unspoilt pastoral flavour of the surrounding countryside, and seeing at first hand a number of small farming communities combine to make this a pleasant outing.

Holwick Fell

START The drinking fountain, Middleton-in-Teesdale, DL12 0SH, GR NY947254

DISTANCE 9½ miles/15.3km with 1,250ft/380m of ascent

SUMMARY A difficult walk mainly on field, riverside and moorland paths

MAPS OS Explorer OL31 North Pennines; OS Landranger 92 Barnard Castle & Richmond

PARKING Roadside parking in Middleton-in-Teesdale

WHERE TO EAT AND DRINK Various places in Middleton-in-Teesdale

A walk over the high moors to the south-west of Middleton-in-Teesdale.

From the drinking fountain go left along Bridge St, following this down over the County Bridge to join the Pennine Way (**1**). Go right along this between the telephone exchange and the cattle market. Keep on over fields and meadows to reach the footbridge over Eel Beck. Cross this and the stile beyond onto the banks of the River Tees. Go left, upstream, and continue to the arched wooden footbridge of Scoberry (**2**).

Leave the Pennine Way here and go left over a stile, then right to pass through a gap in the stone wall, going left up across two fields to the road. Turn right and walk along the road through Holwick village to where it turns a sharp 90-degree right. Leave the road and go left along a track towards a house. Pass this and where the track forks, keep left. When the track levels out, go steeply down to the left to cross a stream, and then climb up through the rocky outcrops to reach a gate. Go through this and continue ahead to another gate. Keep straight ahead to reach a stream, cross this and keep on to a second one. Cross this and go through a gate on the other side, following the wall on the right uphill. The path will then head left away from the wall over open moors to reach a gate through a wall (**3**).

Keep on the track over the moors to a gate in a fence. Go through this and keep along the track through Rake Gill, and then after a gate keep left where the track forks to join the Pennine Way at a gate (**4**).

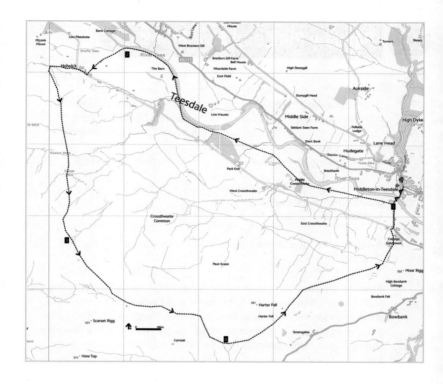

Go left along the Pennine Way. Follow it over Harter Fell initially towards Kirkcarrion, with good views over Lunedale, before dropping down to join the Holwick road beside a house. Go right, then immediately left along the B6277 to the cattle market (**1**). Retrace your outward route back to the drinking fountain.

Points of interest

Holwick consists of a few houses spread along a road in the pattern of a linear settlement.

100 Pawlaw Pike and Five Pikes

START Lay-by on B6278, DL13 2TA, GR NY996307

DISTANCE 9¾ miles/15.7km with 1,500ft/455m of ascent

SUMMARY A difficult walk mainly on good paths/tracks; navigation could be difficult in poor visibility

MAPS OS Explorer OL31 North Pennines; OS Landranger 92 Barnard Castle & Richmond

PARKING Roadside parking

WHERE TO EAT AND DRINK None

A walk over the remote heather moorlands between Teesdale and Weardale.

From the parking area, walk north along the B6278 and take the vehicle track going off on the right, following it as far as a parking area. Go left along a grassy track, following it towards Long Man, and just after passing a grouse butt go right at a small cairn. Follow the narrow path through the heather towards Pawlaw Pike. Join a vehicle track to the left of Pawlaw Pike, going right along it as far as a cairn on the left. At a sharp right turn, leave the track here and continue along the path through heather over the slopes of Five Pikes to reach some trees beside a wall **(1)**.

Go right along the wall, aiming towards Elephant Trees in the distance. You don't actually reach the trees, though; only follow the wall as far as the track coming up to a gate through the wall. Here, go right across pathless heather to the trig point, keeping on in the same direction still over pathless heather to descend to the confluence of two streams. Go right over North Grain Beck and follow this down to the Meeting O' Grains. There are the ruins of an old farm here; pass these and go through a gate to ford South Grain Beck **(2)**.

After crossing the stream go right uphill along a path through the heather, and follow this to a gate on Black Hill. Go through this to enter Hamsterley Forest, going straight ahead along a forest track. Cross a forest road and keep on downhill in the same direction. At the next

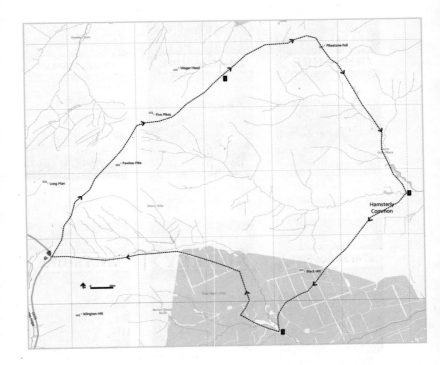

forest road, cross and go slightly left onto a steep path that leads down to a stream (3).

Ford the stream and go left to a forest road, going right along it. Keep right at a junction to reach a gate at the edge of the forest. Go through this and continue ahead along the track through Sharnberry Gill to return to the parking area.

Points of interest

Hamsterley Forest is the largest forest in County Durham and covers more than 2,000 hectares.

OTHER TITLES IN THIS SERIES

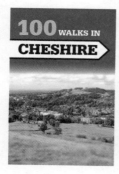

978 1 78500 181 9

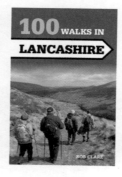

978 1 84797 899 8

978 1 78500 183 3

978 1 78500 347 9

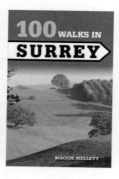

978 1 78500 302 8

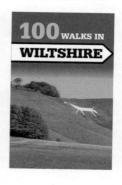

978 1 78500 043 0

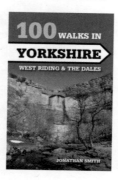

978 1 84797 909 4